Who's Negotiating Your Next Vehicle Purchase/Lease

An instructional work by the author and research team at

Creative Automobile Information.com

Dedication

To my family and friends who have believed and pressured for the writing of this instructional book in order to accurately convey this information so that all of our readers can enjoy the same benefits we have been enjoying for over 25 years of car buying and negotiating.

For my dear friends Alvin and Susan Stein, who have entrusted me with their automobile needs and advice for many years. Susan has also done a remarkable job of editing this manuscript so that all readers can seamlessly understand all of the concepts and skills necessary to;

"Negotiate their next Vehicle Purchase/Lease."

While every precaution has been taken in the preparation of this book, the author assumes no responsibility for errors or omissions, or for damages resulting from the use of the information contained herein.

Copyright © 2007 Scott J Nichol. All rights reserved
ISBN 978-0-6151-8247-6
Library of Congress Control Number: 2008920444

By Creative Automobile Information.Com

Table of Contents

Preface _____ v

Chapter 1   Getting Started with Your Purchase _____ 1

Chapter 2   Which Vehicle is Right For You _____ 11

Chapter 3   Affordability _____ 21

Chapter 4   Choosing Where to Buy Your Car _____ 33

Chapter 5   Negotiating the Deal, Step by Step _____ 41

Chapter 6   Trading in Your Old Car _____ 51

Chapter 7   Final Negotiations _____ 59

Chapter 8   The Delivery Process _____ 65

Glossary of Purchase Terms _____ 69

Glossary of Lease Terms _____ 81

Dealer Slang Terms _____ 105

Preface

Congratulations on taking the first step in acquiring your new or used car! When you're ready to buy or lease, our books will point you in the right direction. Whether you decide on buying privately, using an auto broker or consultant, going through an established online service or going at it alone at your local dealer. Our knowledge and experience will help you find a vehicle that meets your needs for a price you're willing to pay.

A lot has changed in 35 years. Today's vehicles last twice as long as the cars of the 70's but they cost ten times as much. Today the median price of a new car is $25,500 dollars. According to the US Department of Transportation, today's vehicles will average 145,000 miles in 13 years. So as you can see, your negotiations and the value you create in this purchase will be with you for some time if you decide to purchase. If you decide to lease, you will still enjoy money saving strategies for the best possible outcome of your lease expenses.

Thirty five years ago, used car buyers dreamed of buying new cars, while new car buyers dreamed of more expensive models. Now, many smart car shoppers who want quality and dependability are turning to used cars first. There are plentiful supplies of warranted, low mileage, late model cars coming off lease, which have altered both the new and used car marketplace. With yearly model changes a thing of the past, most of these well maintained, late model vehicles look and perform like new.

Don't wait until the last minute to go shopping, whether it's new or used. If you don't take your time, salespeople can pressure you into making bad decisions. An anxious or desperate buyer is the car dealer's best friend.

Primarily there are 4 ways to purchase a vehicle. Let's say you go to a dealer in your area and look around. Spotting a vehicle you like, you enter the showroom. You sit down with the first available salesperson, agree on a monthly payment that sounds affordable, sign a purchase order and give them a deposit. The next day the dealer calls you and says your loan has been approved. He/She tells you when you can pick the car up. This method provides a simple, quick and painless sales experience for you and an unexpected windfall for the lucky dealer. Chances are you settled on a vehicle you knew little about, paying $500 to $3000 more for it than you had to. Unfortunately this is the way many Americans buy cars.

Secondly, you can hire an auto broker. Brokers can find a car matching your specifications, get the best financing, negotiate for you and deliver the vehicle to you. If you have a trade, they'll find a buyer for it as well. As you might imagine this is quite expensive.

Thirdly, the online buying method is quickly becoming the preferred method for busy people who don't have the time to do any comparison shopping at multiple dealerships. If you're easily intimidated by salespeople or dread dealer negotiations, we recommend online buying for you. This method provides a simple, quick and painless sales experience, without the fear of being pressured by a salesperson or business manager. The online buying experience is essentially the same as using a reputable auto broker. The only thing you need to worry about is deciding which vehicle is right for you. Online buyers get competitive prices, while the participating dealers benefit by trimming sales commissions and marketing expenses. This is the way most Americans will purchase their vehicles in the next ten years.

If you're up for the challenge, the fourth and most satisfying way to buy a new or used car is for you to do your own research and negotiations. By studying this material you can effectively make a smart, informed decision about which car is right for you. You'll learn to get your financing before you buy. You'll become familiar with leasing, warranties and insurance. You'll use dealer inventories for hands on evaluation and test driving.

After narrowing your search, you'll begin negotiations. If you decide on a used car, you will learn how to check these cars for reliability and then go on to final negotiations and buy your car.

As with all decision making processes, preparation is the key for getting good results. In the automobile business, knowledge is power. Our proven method helps you, the consumer; navigate the waters of the automotive marketplace. With the exception of the physical inspection, you'll use the same process whether the car you want is new or used.

Consider these questions. What does your vehicle need to do for you? What are your available choices and options?

Do your homework and review the various types of cars, trucks and hybrids available, safety features, front-wheel drive versus rear-wheel drive versus all-wheel drive, manual versus automatic transmission, optional equipment and many other considerations.

This is where you will narrow your choices to a few cars that suit your needs. If you just want a car that suits your desire than you can apply all of these variables, just in a different context, NEED versus DESIRE.

As most of you already know, the down payment and the monthly installments aren't the only costs of owning an automobile. To see what amount of money you can realistically afford to put into your car, make a budget early while deciding your needs for your next car. If you need to finance your car, use a payment calculator to see how changes in rate, purchase price, terms and down payment can reduce your loan payments.

Valuable shopping advice and price information online helps you refine your choices further. You can literally become an expert on the cars on your list, what options they come with and how much they sell for in your area. It's easy to find a like-new car for substantially less money. Consider a used car if your budget doesn't allow for what you really need in a new car. You can research the used cars history and get a good perspective of how well this car will suit your needs using online sources like Kbb.Com (Kelly Blue Book) and CARFAX to name a few.

To get a good deal, get your financing pre-approvals first. If you have no idea what your credit report shows, now is the time to order a credit report from FreeCreditReport.com. See what's in your report before you speak to any car dealer or financial institution.

Web-based lenders provide more options for internet-savvy loan shoppers and can help you get financing. Bankruptcies, bad or non-existent credit are no longer a problem for most customers, providing they have a steady income. Just fill out the applications online to see if you qualify.

Leasing is a good idea for businesses, salespeople, or people who can deduct the payments on their tax returns (Consult your tax adviser for eligibility first). Leasing offers lower payments than conventional financing, because you are not buying the car for its total purchase price. Instead, you are paying for its depreciation for the amount of time of the lease, and being taxed on that total figure only.

You will learn what to look for in a dealer and how high pressure sales teams can work to your benefit, as long as you stay cool and don't react to an impulse buying situation. A salesperson is trained to remove objections so you will be trained to not reveal your objections and remain uncommitted to any one vehicle. Remember, the best negotiator is the one who can always walk away from the table. We hope you will always remember these words as you negotiate fairly with any salesperson.

And finally, know what to look out for during the delivery process. All terms of a financial deal will come together here and usually can not be reversed after you take delivery. You will learn to take notes about all of the financing, accessories and warranties that will be included in your purchase and make sure that nothing comes up unexpected at delivery. Again, if your car is out front, all shined up with your license plates already attached, it is very common to accept any "minor" change in the deal. This is when you will have to stay strongest and walk away from the table leaving your car to the next customer.

So lets get started learning how to buy or lease your next vehicle, and you will be the one, "Negotiating Your Next Vehicle/Purchase".

Chapter 1 *Getting Started with Your Purchase*

Alright, you decided to take on this car buying venture on your own and now you're going to be educated on how to do this without losing your mind and your wallet. The best thing is to start at the beginning and understand exactly what you're going to do and the people that you have to contact to do it.

The people involved in your purchase on the face side are you, the banker and the dealer. It sounds pretty easy to contend with, right? Well, not so fast! Buying a car to the banker is just like buying real estate. The banker determines the value of your purchase and lends money and adjusts the rate of return based on its value versus your down payment (your equity). Good news is if you buy from a dealer who is also providing or shopping for the financing, they will be in a better position to get you approved at a fair rate.

Well, not exactly. They will act as agent for the lender and the lender pays them for their services (see below about different income sources). The dealership also has other people or entities in their corner. They are you, the purchaser, their affiliated banker or their own financial subsidiary for lending money. If this is a new car purchase the manufacturer is also involved.

While the dealer may stand a better chance of getting you approved it's only because of the volume of business that they do with the financial institution(s). In return for this volume they are allowed to quote a rate higher than that of the banks offering and the dealership is paid a bonus for the difference. We'll call this income source #1. Now they have priced the car at or slightly below Manufacturer's Suggested Retail Price (MSRP). You think that's a good deal. But there are thousands of dollars between dealer invoice and MSRP and that becomes income source #2. Then of course the extended warranty and the accessories that you would like to add on at delivery all come to be income source #3. Lastly, the dealership has another income source from the manufacturer in the form of incentives, volume discounts and holdback. (Income source #4)

The idea of negotiating the best price for a car shouldn't be to eliminate any of the sources of income that the dealership gets, after all the dealer has a lot of people on his/her payroll, commissions to be paid out to salespeople, financing charges on inventory, building expenses and so on. But as an educated consumer you will be able to lessen some of the charges from that purchase.

First, we will start with the bank. If you were to shop before hand for a lender; you could very possibly save thousands over the life of the loan, because there is no provider or broker to be paid. The bank can offer you very competitive rates. Just don't reveal this to the dealers as you are shopping for the vehicle and negotiating its price, just leave it as an "undecided decision" when it comes up, or maybe you want to say "depends on the deal".

You will need to check your states Office of Consumer Affairs regarding truth in lending clauses of when you are committed to buy. For instance, in some states if you don't reveal your intentions of not using their provided finance company you have up until the offering of rate and terms to back out of a signed purchase agreement. This offering of rate and terms should also be the delivery, but we will talk about that in detail in Chapter 8. So, it is important for you to leave the decision on the provider of financing open because most states truth in lending laws do not apply when you are not financing through the dealer. This applies to new or used purchases. It is very important for you to know the law and how it will relate to your negotiations and purchases.

Having a firm commitment from a lending institution is going to do a couple of things for you. First, it will determine the guidelines for the price of the car that you can afford; this information will help you with your affordability worksheets in chapter 3. Second, is that you won't be interested in negotiating your sale as a monthly payment. You need to stay focused on the actual sales price of the car. This will also apply to lease negotiations as well, because a lease payment is very definitely calculated from a total sale price, regardless of what a salesperson might tell you.

Next we're going to talk about MSRP. (Manufacturer's Suggested Retail Price.) Suggested being the operative word meaning the dealership has the right to accept or decline any offer for its inventory. So if you're looking at the newest convertible sport model of which there was only 5,000 produced by the manufacturer, than you may be surprised that this negotiation may not move off of MSRP at all. That's because supply and demand will determine what the dealer will accept. But this can work for you if your interested in that funky colored sedan with a standard shift transmission that's been sitting on the dealer's lot all year long. See what I mean?

There are online pricing websites that will help you find dealers invoices on the cars you want. For instance, Kbb.com (Kelley Blue Book) is a very good and reliable resource. Here you will be able to enter the year, make, model and options for a new car and the website will calculate dealer invoice and MSRP as well it will search for the most current programs available for that car in your area. Play around with this in different areas because $2,500 in rebates or incentives may be worth traveling for if they can be applied to your purchase or lease. Try to find out this information using the dealer's websites. Their internet sales managers will be happy to answer your questions. Remember, once you have what is believed to be, the dealer's invoice price, you want your negotiations to target that number as close as possible. Subtract the rebates from the dealer's invoice and that's your target. Kbb.com can also provide very accurate pricing of used cars in your area as long as you understand their website settings for vehicle condition.

Be careful about the dealer's presentation of the deal. They may offer a deal very close to invoice or your target, but it may require your securing financing at their participating lender. This may put the terms and rates out of your control. You can ask that the stipulation of financing be removed from the offer as you have not decided on how to finance your purchase or who will be providing the financing for the lease. Or you can accept this offer conditionally upon presentation of terms regardless of your states truth in lending laws. Remember your first priority in negotiations is the final purchase price, even if you decide to lease; this price sets up the payments for the lease. Use a purchase versus lease calculator at Edmunds.com to see how the base price can affect your monthly payments. If your bank participates, they too can purchase the car and lease it back to you. This is a complex structure of a deal, but the main elements remain the same. Ask your bank if they provide 3rd party leasing to their customers.

Then we have the extended warranties and accessories. There is an awful lot of room for negotiating with this subject. First, let's examine the extended warranty. Why would you need an extended warranty on a vehicle that already is offered with a comprehensive warranty? Know and understand the terms of the vehicles warranty before you step into the Finance and Insurance Office (F&I) of the dealership. You can get all of this information from the manufacturer's websites or Kbb.com. This way you can determine the value of insuring something that's already covered by the manufacturer. Keep in mind the amount of time you choose to have possession of the car and how long you plan to finance your purchase. Don't purchase an extended warranty on a car you are going to lease for 36 months if it already has a warranty of 3 years/36,000 miles bumper to bumper coverage. As well you don't want to be financing that same car for 5 years without warranty coverage of the last 2 years of payments due. Don't buy an extended policy to reduce an interest rate. This should not have any bearing on that interest rate. This process is a sales tactic in the F&I office. For example, if you have been quoted a finance rate of 9% annually for an amount of $25,000, but are offered a reduction to 8% if you purchase an extended warranty policy, chances are good this 8% was available to you anyway. So insist on that rate regardless and maybe even a lower rate depending on your offers that you secured beforehand. See how your education of the process can save you thousands?

Accessories, first there are usually option packages available from the manufacturer that has been researched to the buying public's wants and needs. As well these accessories or options have been designed into the vehicle and will be an integral part of the vehicle adding greater value in the future of this cars resale value. If the dealer is attempting to add-on any accessories that weren't installed by the manufacturer but are "just as good" insist on seeing their installations and comparing them to original equipment by the manufacturer (OEM) and how they will be warranted. Some add-on accessories are very good quality and can be installed with great levels of skill, but unfortunately that is not the case in all aftermarket installations. Lastly, concerning aftermarket installations, most accessories that effectively change the intended operation of some or all of a vehicles operation may void that portion of its warrantee if it is found to have failed as a result of such modification. So choose your accessories carefully. Remember, even if it is installed by the manufacturer's dealer or its agent it may not be covered by another dealer should it need to be serviced.

Let's understand how all of this so far relates to your purchase through an example of a typical visit to the dealership. You arrive at the dealership and are browsing a specific model with the option packages that you desire. You have already made a decision about what you would like to purchase, through the manufacturer's website and a salesperson approaches you. You exchange greetings and he immediately senses that you have already researched the car that suits you and he invites you inside to check stock and availability for these option packages. On the way into the showroom the salesperson asks, "Have you decided whether you want to purchase or lease? Will you be financing your purchase?" At this time you should be very careful not to reveal your intentions because a definitive answer to any one of these can stop the individual base price negotiations and gear your negotiations to payments and terms. Make it clear in polite terms that you're **Mainly Interested** in the purchase price of the vehicle.

So you have the basic information about dealer's invoice and incentives or rebates available for this car in your area and you start negotiating a price that you are willing to pay. **STOP** and do not reveal what you are willing to pay, otherwise that monthly payment or base price payment will be magically achieved in the end of negotiations and the salesperson will use that as a removal of objection to your taking delivery when he/she says, "I brought your payment to exactly what you wanted I can't do any better than that." Instead you might make your own offer on paper and let the salesperson present it to his management. Your offer will most likely not include financing terms just base price. Even the down payment is not the dealer's concern until the purchase price is agreed upon. If you come to an agreement make sure it is written clearly and accompanies all documents that follow the rest of the process.

We're not done yet, we need to choose the car that's right for you and determine if it's affordable. This chapter covered the first steps because the results of the next chapters depend on your knowledge of the whole car buying/leasing experience.

Chapter 2 *Which Vehicle is Right for You?*

You now have a good understanding of the processes that are involved in your purchase or lease. With that knowledge we are going to show you how to shop for your vehicle based on your needs, because the processes, needs and affordability will go hand in hand.

First, let's understand the difference between needs and wants. You may **need** a seven passenger minivan because of your frequent trips driving your children and their friends back and forth to sporting events. But you **want** that two-seater convertible in red because of your frequent trips driving your children and their friends back and forth to sporting events. Well this example is obvious to the differences in needs and wants, but little differences in vehicles can help you understand why buying the wrong car is a mistake. This will help you understand what you should choose and what your priorities are. You can't get seven people and their gear into a four passenger sedan just as much as you can't change the SUV's mileage ratings after winter is over and you don't require four wheel drive anymore. So think carefully about your needs now and into the future as we explore the different types of vehicles available.

If you already know something about cars, trucks or vans, write down all the ones you might like to have. Skip ones you can't afford, for instance maybe: Ferraris, Bentleys, Lamborghinis, or Rolls-Royces!

As you read your list consider how these cars will fit with your life and budget. If you don't know what kind of car you want yet, don't worry. We'll just continue on to your needs. Your car should suit your life-style. That means it fits your budget and can do the jobs you need it to do, while being safe and comfortable.

What does your car need to do for you? You may need a car for work or you or your spouse might need a second car. Some of you are looking for a status symbol, while others might need to replace a family sedan in the last days of its useful life. Depending on their recreational activities, singles and young couples might desire a sports car, convertible or pick-up truck. Active families will want to consider a station wagon or minivan. Many people want to buy an SUV. If you own a motorcycle, travel-trailer, or boat, a large heavy-duty pickup truck may be necessary. A snowy climate or hilly terrain may require an all-wheel-drive vehicle. People living in the desert or high in the mountains may need a full-time four-wheel-drive SUV if off-road or severe-weather excursions are necessary.

Think twice before allowing your inexperienced teenager to drive a tiny car. Drivers under 20 account for a very high percentage of traffic fatalities, so consider the safety of a large or mid-sized sedan for young drivers. Smaller 4-cylinder vehicles offer good fuel economy and maneuverability in urban environments, while 6-cylinder engines are better for interstate travelers. You should give careful consideration to your family's ages, life-styles, occupations and hobbies when choosing a car.

Shared Platforms, Platform means a vehicle's suspension, drive train, and structural components. Large manufacturers with multiple divisions produce similar models under different nameplates. GM, Ford and Chrysler realize that brand loyalty remains an important factor in North American marketing, so look for the domestic siblings and twins to continue for the immediate future. There are numerous examples of shared platforms and look-alike siblings in all vehicle areas. The world's automotive industry increasingly depends on shared platforms. They enable manufacturers to market essentially identical vehicles to different market segments, to help recoup research and development costs. Manufacturers sometimes share development costs and facilities, resulting in model twins and even triplets.

Safety should be your most important consideration when looking for a new or used motor vehicle. We strongly recommend that you visit the National Highway and Traffic Safety Administration (NHTSA) early in the car-buying process to get the safety rating for the cars you are considering. Every year they publish crash-test results from the Federal Government's New Car Assessment Program (NCAP) and the Insurance Institute for Highway Safety (IIHS). In addition to the most current information, they feature safety data on older cars which lets you assess used cars. You may want to divide safety into three categories: the weight of a vehicle, passive safety features that help people stay alive and uninjured in a crash and active safety features that help drivers avoid accidents. Larger heavier cars with poor ratings may easily produce better results than smaller cars with good ratings. In addition to a car that crashes well (Passive Safety), you should look for a car that can avoid a crash altogether (Active Safety).

Four-wheel-drive pick-up trucks and sport utility vehicles (SUVs) are designed to be driven for work, hauling, and off-road purposes. They were not designed to be people movers and don't handle nearly as well as passenger cars or mini vans. The National Highway Traffic Safety Administration (NHTSA) reports that SUVs are four times more likely to roll over than passenger cars in high-speed maneuvers. In addition, SUV to car collisions are six times more likely to kill the occupants of the smaller vehicle when compared to a normal car-to-car collision. You may be safer inside an SUV, but you're at greater risk of killing others in the event of an accident.

All cars must meet US Department of Transportation standards for crash-worthiness. Larger and heavier cars, however, are usually safer in a collision than smaller ones. If a heavier vehicle collides head-on with a lighter one, the lighter will suffer substantially more damage. Large cars offer increased levels of comfort and roominess when compared to their smaller siblings, and today's fuel injected engines allow mid-sized, 6-cylinder automobiles to enjoy remarkably good gas mileage.

Restraint systems are also crucial. Safety belts are the best safety device ever developed for the automobile. First installed in the 1950s, they have been mandatory equipment since 1967. Initial use was low (20% in 1970), but education and legislation increased their usage to over 70% by 1987. Modern restraints have automatic seat-belt pre-tensioners to pick up the slack and stretch that occurs in an accident, providing better occupant protection and additional space for the airbag deployment.

It's important to remember that even though airbags help reduce serious injuries, safety belts are still needed for full protection. Seat belts and airbags work together in a collision. Driver and passenger-side airbags are now standard equipment on every new motor vehicle sold in the US. Most used cars made after 1996 have them as well. Side-impact airbags greatly increase protection.

Most automobile headrests provide little protection in rear-end accidents. European automobiles rate far better than domestic or Asian models in this area. The federal government required their installation in 1967, but hasn't provided standards for their successful implementation. An effective headrest is one that's directly behind the centerline of the head and positioned no more than a couple of inches away. Structural integrity is another important component of passive safety. The US Department of Transportation requires that the doors and passenger compartments of automobiles made after 1996 meet minimal side impact standards.

Active safety features help drivers avoid accidents. A vehicle's tires, brakes, handling, acceleration and visibility all make important contributions to active crash avoidance. The most important safety items on a car are the tires. Think about it: they're all that connects your vehicle to the road. A good set of tires can make a huge difference to the way a car responds to emergency maneuvers. Tire quality also noticeably affects the way a car handles. Sport touring tires have much more grip than regular tires, although their softer compounds don't last as long. Anti-lock brakes (ABS) are an often-misunderstood active safety feature. ABS helps you maintain steering control while braking, especially on slippery surfaces. Take time to understand how it works because in an abrupt stop, ABS feels noticeably different. With regular brakes, sudden stops tend to lock up the brakes, causing a skid. Anti-lock brakes sense when a wheel is locked and electronically pump the brakes ten times faster than you could do it, making a ratcheting noise and a vibration in the brake pedal. Old braking techniques must be unlearned in order to use ABS effectively. In a panic stop, depress the brake pedal once, and hold it down firmly. Do not pump the pedal as you normally would, because that defeats the system. Traction Control is an option that improves traction and directional stability on slippery roads, using a combination of electronics, drive train control, and ABS. Some systems adjust engine power output while gently applying the brakes to particular wheels during acceleration and cornering. If not already standard, most of these features are usually combined in a "preferred equipment" group. Try to think of ABS as stability while braking and traction control as stability while accelerating.

Look for cup-holders located away from important vehicle controls (heat, vents, AC, radio). Make sure that they're sturdy and can securely hold a beverage in the event of a sudden stop or accident avoidance maneuver. Tilt or adjustable steering wheels are another item usually found as standard equipment. They enable different-sized drivers to reposition the steering wheel for comfort and safety, allowing the instrument panel to be visible at all times.

If you do any expressway driving, cruise control is beneficial. Cruise control reduces driver fatigue on long journeys; in addition to keeping your insurance rates low by helping to avoid speeding tickets. A power adjustable driver's seat is another device that should be standard on every vehicle. Look for a driver's seat with adjustable lumbar support as well. On long trips, the comfort of the driver is an often forgotten safety consideration. Combined with an adjustable steering column and remote control mirrors, adjustable seating offers good visibility to any sized driver. Remote control power adjustable left and right side mirrors enable different drivers to see the traffic around them, no matter what their driving position. Central-locking and remote keyless entry systems allow the driver to lock and unlock all the doors from one location, improving safety as well as adding convenience. Power windows may be necessary for toll highway users or if you use parking lots or garages requiring a card or code for entry.

If peace of mind, trouble-free driving, and a high level of reliability are important factors for you, a late model or new vehicle may be necessary. New car warranties are more comprehensive, backed by solid companies and last for longer periods of time than the extended warranties you may get with a used car. According to consumer polling organizations, Acura, Honda, Lexus, Toyota and Mercedes-Benz produce the most reliable vehicles in today's new and used car marketplace. Don't rule out American and European manufacturers, as their reliability has increased tremendously in the past 10 years.

Remember, a reliable car will only stay that way as long as you maintain it properly.

EPA gas mileage results are listed on the window stickers of all new vehicles. You can find EPA ratings for all cars and calculate their costs per year for fuel by simply dividing the EPA rating into the expected miles driven per year (Usually 12,000- 15,000 per year) That will be your yearly amount of gallons necessary on an average to travel your intended amount of miles. Then you will multiply that number by your current average price per gallon to arrive at your yearly costs for fuel. For example, if the car I'm contemplating is rated at 24 miles per gallon average and I intend to drive it 12,000 miles per year than I will require 500 gallons of fuel per year, multiplied by my average price per gallon of $3.05 equals $1,525.00 average cost of fuel per year. We're not suggesting that you shop on gas mileage alone, but be aware of more fuel-efficient alternatives.

Performance has become an important safety feature for modern drivers. A responsive gas pedal allows you another option (brake or accelerate) when an accident unfolds before you. Good performance allows you to pass slow moving vehicles on country roads, and to merge into fast-moving feeder lanes on expressways. Fast thinking and a responsive throttle can help you to avoid an accident that a slower vehicle couldn't.

When evaluating a vehicle, take a close look at the engine size (expressed in liters), the number of cylinders (4, 6 or 8), and the engine's power output (expressed in horsepower).

Drive some of these at your local dealers even if it's just to get the feel of the different amounts of performance or the amount of visibility or your ability to park this size vehicle. Do not consider a vehicle that seems too powerful or overbearing or generally not comfortable driving. Only you can make these decisions. Make lists explaining likes and dislikes of all the vehicles that come close to your needs and filter these lists into affordability in the next chapter.

Chapter 3 *Affordability*

This step outlines some of the best and worst ways to pay for your motor vehicle purchase. It recommends making a realistic budget to find out what you can afford and summarizes the hidden costs of ownership. If you must drive, (and most of us must) you can eliminate the costs associated with financing and leasing entirely, reduce tax and maintenance costs considerably and keep your expenses to a minimum, by following this simple advice; buy used vehicles in excellent condition that are two to three years old and always pay cash for them. Motor vehicle ownership has become a rite of passage to some, and an addiction to others. The hidden costs, personal, societal and global, make it costlier than it seems. The rest of this section itemizes the costs connected with buying and then owning a car.

Make a budget. This is absolutely essential. It's the only smart way to prepare to buy a car. You need to know how much money you can spend without compromising your finances. First determine your income, then your expenses without an automobile. Subtract your expenses from your income. What's left is your disposable income or the amount available for entertainment, travel and automotive expenses. Don't forget, these expenses will include the hidden costs of car ownership.

We have provided a comprehensive vehicle financing analysis worksheet for your use, at the end of this chapter.

Low or no interest rate teasers, desperate to unload slow-moving inventory, many manufacturers are offering the best deals in history, providing you have excellent credit and finance through the automaker's finance company. If you qualify, take advantage of these incredible financing deals. Unfortunately many new car purchasers won't qualify for the lowest rate. The dealers will qualify your credit score into tiers and offer rates dependant on your score. It is very difficult to reach a Tier 1 unless you don't need the financing to begin with. At which time you probably don't want to finance the car and you will eliminate all of the costs associated with financing your purchase.

If you need to finance, use a payment calculator to see how changes in rate, purchase price, term and down payment can reduce your loan payments. Longer financing periods (60 & 72 month loans are common) enable many people to buy more car (newer or better) than they can really afford. The longer loan term includes far more interest than shorter loans. Banks will want a history of your work experience, a history of your previous residences and history of good credit (paying bills on time, etc). Banks can easily make your financial situation seem better than it really is and qualify you for a loan that will be a burden to repay. Banks calculate your ability to borrow from your debt to income ratio, considering your mortgage/rent and credit obligations.

Borrowers must have a good credit history in order to motivate lenders to part with their money at a reasonable rate. Your credit history is the most significant contributing factor. A person with an excellent repayment history (no late payments) is considered a good credit risk and may enjoy a rate as low as 6%. Another person buying a similar vehicle could pay as much as 20% if their credit history is poor. Keep in mind that interest is in addition to the original price and can add as much as 35% to your total cost. If you have no credit history or your credit report is poor, you may be required to have a co-signer or personal guarantor for your loan. Technically the co-signer is taking the loan out for you, but you are making the payments. Be very careful about borrowing money for a depreciating product on someone else's obligation. Get a copy of your credit report before you go any further. Correct any discrepancies immediately; this will affect your ability to negotiate for the best of terms.

Down payments, most people will need a down payment (for a loan) or capital cost reduction (for a lease) in order to qualify for the loan or lease. By reducing what you owe, your payment will be lowered, so make as large a down payment as you can possibly afford. If you already own a car and are considering using it as a trade this can be a sizeable down payment that has already been taxed on its value, (See your tax professional about the tax savings of a trade in.) assuming you don't owe a balance for financing this car which is now a trade-in. If you own this trade-in but are still making payments, be very careful of a situation called poor percentage of loan to value. When you bought that car it may have been worth the complete amount financed, but has since depreciated, sometimes at a rate greater than your ability to repay. This is known to be "Upside down in your payments or obligation." Some dealers are offering guaranteed approval regardless of what you owe but beware that the differences in equity and payment balances owed will be attached to your new financial agreement making you almost definitely "Upside down before you even take delivery." This isn't terrible if you can easily afford the payments and plan to have the car long after the finance term. But keep in mind what can happen if the car is wrecked in collision where it is deemed to be a total loss or stolen and not recovered. You may be liable for the difference in value your insurance company paid the lender and the balance due on the note immediately upon settlement.

Some of the hidden costs or not so hidden costs are your monthly payment, interest, sales tax and insurance. Don't forget fuel, maintenance and repairs. At delivery you are responsible for the bank fees, sales tax and registration. You can also count on having inspection and emissions fees, which can range from $40 to $600 annually, depending on where you live and what you drive. Finally your insurance costs. Liability insurance is required to register a vehicle, while collision and comprehensive are mandatory when someone is financing your purchase or when leasing. Insurance may be between $50 and $500 a month to be budgeted depending on your zip code, age, gender, marital status, your driving record and your tickets & accidents, as well as the year, make, model and type of vehicle you're insuring. Before you settle on a specific model check with your insurance agent to see how much it will cost for you to insure it.

Maintenance costs will vary with the type of car that you choose and will increase as you buy in the high end market or the older higher mileage cars, (oil changes, tune-ups, tires, brakes, exhaust, car washes) and repairs (heating, air conditioning, cooling system, engine, transmission and driveline). Figure on $30 per month for the first few years of a new car's life. With a used vehicle, figure a little more, about $50 per month. Repair costs are easy to budget on a new car. You won't have any repair costs until the factory warranty runs out (in 3 years or 36,000 miles, typically).

Used cars are a different story. A smart buyer will budget $50 a month for repairs on a late-model used car (less than 5 years old and less than 80,000 miles) and if those amounts are not needed hopefully the amounts will be saved up for a more pressing emergency repair that was unexpected. Older used cars (more than 5 years old and more than 80,000 miles) will need a little more money set aside, say $75 per month. Remember, add the maintenance and repair totals together: budget new autos at $30 per month, late-model used cars at $100 per month, (less if it has a warranty) older used vehicles at $125 per month.

Depreciation costs, your purchase will likely depreciate faster than any other purchase you'll ever make. The first year depreciation on a new automobile can be as high as 35%. On most vehicles it levels out to between 7% & 10% per year after the first three years. Some models can depreciate faster and while others can hold value longer. This information will be helpful when you're shopping for a car to lease because the lease payments are based on rent and depreciation. Find out your car's rate of depreciation, it's the difference in the Manufacturer's Suggested Retail Price (MSRP) and its price at a later time, or residual value. It's usually expressed as a percentage, and it can change from year to year.

Buying a new car is a better choice if peace of mind, trouble free driving and a high level of reliability are important factors for you. New car warranties are more comprehensive, backed by solid companies and last for longer periods than the extended warranties that come with used cars. The comfort levels of owning a new car are important to some buyers. Some people hold on to a vehicle for a long time, eight to ten years. By buying a car or truck new from the factory, you can be sure it gets the proper attention and maintenance that can help it give its owners good service into the future. Buying new gives you more control over the optional features.

Buying a used vehicle also has many advantages; some of the best are when you're on a fixed income and can't afford a new car or regular payments or when you can buy a better used car than any new car you can afford. Used cars provide more flexibility to choose a more expensive vehicle or step up to a better model than could be purchased new. If you pay cash you can eliminate the costs associated with financing as well as lowering your insurance costs because you won't have to carry the higher limits required by the lender or the lease company. If you own a home don't be so quick to lower your insurance limits so that you are left vulnerable should you be involved in a serious collision. Consult your insurance agent about keeping yourself well protected. If you're considering a used car make sure to write down the VIN number (Vehicle Identification Number) so that you can order comprehensive research like [CARFAX](). Lemon law cars, salvage vehicles and numerous other hidden conditions can impact the safety and value of your next vehicle. Insurance company records will show if and when your vehicle has been involved in a claim settlement. Previous paint work, collision damage, flood history, theft, fire damage or vandalism all show up by using the insurance industry database.

These kinds of services are invaluable when they turn up. VIN numbers that have been totaled by insurance companies in other states and wind up repaired on a used car lot will usually show up on your CarFax report.

State DMV's and repair shops also keep strict records relating to odometers and mileage when a vehicle is registered and inspected. Vehicles that have had their odometers replaced, cars imported from Canada or Europe, vehicles whose odometers have gone over 100,000 miles, and vehicles that have had their odometers tampered with will all show up by checking these records.

High Mileage Vehicles are plentiful and some are an excellent value and should be considered as a good buy, however, if the car has been poorly maintained and driven in a lot of city driving situations (stop and go) you would probably be best advised to stay away. The more miles a vehicle has on it the shorter its functional life will be no matter how well cared for it was. But since an average car lasts for 145,000 miles, a vehicle with 60,000 miles can still give you six or seven years of useful transportation, if you drive 12,000 to 15,000 miles a year. The big advantage is driving new technology while paying for old. If you are on a limited budget and willing to take a chance, a 1 or 2-year-old high mileage full or mid-sized domestic sedan is one of the best used car values around.

Orphan Cars, avoid orphan cars like the plague! An orphan is a vehicle whose parent company no longer sells or supports their vehicles in this country. Parts and service are nonexistent for many of these orphans.

Use this calculator at Edmunds.com for a basic purchase budget. (Lease versus purchase decision calculator, basic lease calculator or low APR versus cash back calculator.)

4 Car buying calculators at Edmunds.com

VEHICLE FINANCING W[ORKSHEET]

MONTHLY SPENDING PLAN

1. Complete Column 1 based on your current situation. Start with your monthly take-home pay. This is the amount you have left after taxes and other deductions have been made.

   Subtract the amount you need for savings and monthly expenses, including monthly creditor payments.

   The remaining balance is the maximum amount you can afford to put toward the monthly payment for a vehicle and any new related expenses, like car insurance.

2. Complete Column 2 based on your new situation. This column will show your new vehicle payment and adjuments you've made to expenses and credit obligations. Be sure to adjust any expenses, like vehicle maintenance and insurance expenses, which might go up or down when you get a new vehicle.

   The remaining balance in Column 2 will indicate whether you can afford the new vehicle payment and change in expenses projected.

MONTHLY INCOME & SAVINGS	REVISED [1]	CURRENT [2]
Monthly Take-Home Pay	$_____	$_____
Savings	-$_____	-$_____
MONTHLY EXPENSES:		
Mortgage Payment/Rent	-$_____	-$_____
Utilities	-$_____	-$_____
Food	-$_____	-$_____
Transportation	-$_____	-$_____
Insurance (Home, Vehicle, Life)	-$_____	-$_____
Taxes	-$_____	-$_____
Clothing	-$_____	-$_____
Personal	-$_____	-$_____
Entertainment	-$_____	-$_____
Gifts & Contributions	-$_____	-$_____
Education	-$_____	-$_____
Credit Card Payments	-$_____	-$_____
Other Creditor Payments	-$_____	-$_____
Vehicle Payments	-$_____	-$_____
Miscellaneous	-$_____	-$_____
REMAINING BALANCE:	= $_____	= $_____

By Creative Automobile Information.Com

ORKSHEET

SHOP FOR THE BEST DEAL WHEN FINANCING A VEHICLE

Take the time to know and understand all of the terms, conditions and costs to finance a vehicle before you sign the contract. Review and compare the financing terms offered by more than one creditor.

	CREDITOR 1	CREDITOR 2	CREDITOR 3
Negotiated Price of Vehicle	$	$	$
Down Payment	$	$	$
Extended Service Contract (Optional)*	$	$	$
Credit Insurance (Optional)*	$	$	$
Guaranteed Auto Protection (Optional)*	$	$	$
Other Optional* Products _____	$	$	$
Amount Financed	$	$	$
Annual Percentage Rate (APR)	____%	____%	____%
Finance Charge	$	$	$
Length of Contract in Months			
Number of Payments			
Monthly Payment Amount	$	$	$

*Any items that are "optional" are not required for the purchase. If you do not want these items, tell the dealer and do not sign for them.

SAMPLE COMPARISON

This example will help you compare the difference in the monthly payment amount and the total payment amount for a 3-year and a 5-year credit transaction. Generally, longer terms mean lower monthly payments and higher finance charges. Make sure you have enough income available to make the monthly payment by reviewing your monthly spending plan. You'll also need to factor in the cost of car insurance, which may vary depending upon the type of vehicle.

	3 YEARS (36 MONTHS)	5 YEARS (60 MONTHS)
Amount Financed	$ 20,000	$ 20,000
Contract Rate (APR)	8.00%	8.00%
Finance Charges	$ 2,562	$ 4,332
Monthly Payment Amount	$ 627	$ 406
Total of Payments	$ 22,562	$ 24,332
Down Payment	10%	10%

Note: All dollars have been rounded for this illustration. The numbers in this sample are for example purposes only. Actual finance terms may be different and will depend on many factors, including your credit worthiness.

Chapter 4 *Choosing Where to Buy Your Car*

Choosing where to buy your next car should be your next decision, even if you're specifically looking for just a used car. Consider looking at new car dealer's inventory. If price is not your primary concern, franchised dealerships are the best option for finding new and late model used vehicles. All new car dealers carry used cars, because they are more profitable than new cars. New car dealers keep only the best trade-ins and usually give them a thorough inspection. Special manufacturer's auctions, which are only open to franchised dealers, supply their remaining inventory. A dealer who specializes in the brand that you're looking for may be able to furnish maintenance records for particular vehicles, from the manufacturer's shared databases or simply from their own customer records. Look for a dealer with a large inventory, a busy service department, and a well staffed parts counter. Visit as many franchised dealerships as possible and don't be afraid to try out and test drive any vehicle that appeals to you.

Typically the mark up between an independent used car lot (between $2,000.00 and $3,000.00) and a franchised dealer ($4,000.00 and $6,000.00) will be different because of the level of service that they are able to provide. Most used car dealers offer dependable transportation at a reasonable price.

If you're only looking to buy or lease a new car, then visit the dealerships that specialize in the brand or type of vehicle you're looking for. They can be a good source of shopping information in the form of brochures specific to their models, to information regarding incentives and rebates available. If you're still shopping different models you will be able to test drive the different models with different equipment packages installed. Remember most manufacturer franchised dealers are independent retailers that have the ability to charge for their inventory whatever the market will bear. As you enter the different facilities take note at how comfortable you are in their stores, as well as how uncomfortable you become during your inquiries specific to their products. Simply put; if it feels like you are being asked all the questions than chances are they are preparing you for the removal of objections, the primary goal to car sales. You do the asking about products you're considering, your intentions of buying, leasing, trade-in or down payment are not important at this point.

Ask your friends, neighbors, and relatives about the cars they own and question the people you know driving cars that interest you. This can be an easy way to find a good car, since you know the owner and can find out how it was treated. Friends and relatives are usually happy to sell their cars for the amount of their lease buy out or trade-in. So speak up if you're interested in their current car. Make sure any car you acquire this way is thoroughly inspected by an independent mechanic before you finalize any deals. You don't want a problem with this car ruining a friend or family relationship.

Some of the larger rental car companies feature rental car sales divisions. These cars are usually late model, minimally equipped models that have been driven by a variety of different drivers. Some of the rental car companies have very strict service requirements to protect their investments while others may be less than desired. The deals can be very good financially as these cars will normally be at the bottom end of their listed values. But choose carefully and have them inspected by a professional first and ask to see the service records.

Dealer demonstrators are not available very often, and are rarely a good deal. Consider the vehicle a used car, because that's exactly what it is. The dealer has been using it for test drives. Your salesperson will tell you not to consider it a used vehicle because it still has the Manufacturer's Certificate of Origin, and has never been titled or registered. But under the law, a demonstrator is a used vehicle and should be considered as such and researched accordingly.

There's no substitute for going to dealerships for a hands-on evaluation of the cars that you're interested in driving and for sampling different option packages. Unfortunately, many shoppers hesitate. Usually they are unprepared and fearful of paying too much or being coerced into buying something they don't want. To counter this apprehension, manufacturers are trying to make car buying a pleasant experience. Manufacturers now issue consumer relations guidelines that dealers are supposed to follow. Even then, you will be treated differently at every place you visit. The selling style and buying experience at different dealerships is likely a result of the personality of the dealerships owners or management. Owners and managers interested in quick profits are most likely to train their sale people to be a high-pressure sales staff. Laid-back sales staff indicates an owner interested in good customer relations and the profitable referrals good relations bring. In talking with your salesperson you'll get a feeling for the dealership's personality and will quickly find out if you need to go elsewhere. When you enter the dealership look like you're ready to do business. Be polite and feel confident in your preparation and knowledge of the products you have selected. Go to another dealer if you feel you're being mistreated. Remember you are in charge of the process.

Choose a dealership with as much attention as you choose your vehicle. Establish a firm relationship with the dealer you want to purchase from. This will pay off in later years when servicing this car becomes more and more frequent due to its age and use. Vehicles bought and serviced at the same dealer are usually given a service priority when problems arise. Free loaners may be offered to good customers, while rental cars may be the only option for others. You might learn to regret the decision to travel for a $500 difference in price when you have to service your vehicle closer to home. The dealers can find out through their manufacturer's databases where the car was purchased. Look for the showroom and surrounding grounds to be neat and well-organized, with a varied supply of vehicles. The atmosphere and sales staff should be friendly, helpful and polite. Ask to see a copy of the dealership's latest Customer Satisfaction Index (CSI Scores). This report will show how customers rate the dealer's sales and service departments. How the dealership treats you in the showroom can indicate the kind of service help you'll receive once you've purchased the vehicle. You can also call the service department directly and ask the service manager about the shop's CSI score, staffing, turn-over and training. An adequately-staffed parts department suggests a good parts inventory. Clean well-equipped shops with ASE certified technicians are also a plus. Ask the service manager how many technicians have completed factory training programs (should be 90% or higher), and what percentage of his/her mechanics would be considered "A" techs (more than 50% is excellent). No two dealerships will treat you the same, as each is independently owned and operated. To find a nice salesperson, try entering the dealership through the service department. Remember their job is to make a sale, so don't fault them for persistence. But don't let yourself be coerced into a decision during the beginning of your search.

As an educated car shopper, you'll take your time. You'll look at many different makes and models to arrive at your buying decision based on careful analysis and research. This will likely be the opposite of the salesperson's goal of putting you into a car at the highest amount of profit possible. A salesperson tries to qualify, and then spend time with the potential buyers who will make the fastest, most profitable sale. They are looking for eager uneducated buyers, desperate to buy the first thing they set their eyes on. An eager buyer is a poor negotiator and usually ends up paying substantially more than an educated buyer. Since most salespeople are on commission, they make more money if you pay more money. Their goal is to sell you any vehicle in stock, at the highest possible price. Your goal is to get the best vehicle you can find at the lowest possible price.

A successful salesperson concentrates on "buying today." Dealers are convinced that if you don't buy today, they'll never see you again. You can count on a good salesperson to ask you, "What can I do to put you in this car today?" If they can sell you a vehicle today, you won't have the chance to buy it tomorrow from another dealer. This misplaced priority will show up in their CSI scores. In the meantime, keep your own focus clearly on your own goals.

When you go into the showroom, let them know that you're interested in test-driving a car you're considering buying. An experienced salesperson should recognize that you aren't buying today and won't pressure or pester you. If they do, remember their job is to make a sale, so don't fault them for persistence. Assure them that you're seriously considering their vehicle for purchase and if you choose it, they'll be the first to know. Don't let yourself be coerced into a purchase during the beginning of your search. Politely make it clear that you are there for a test drive.

Some dealers require that a guest sheet be filled out prior to test driving. Do not reveal all of your intentions, basic name, phone numbers and type of vehicle you're looking for should be plenty of information. Don't sign anything or furnish any credit information. They will also require a copy of your driver's license before you drive their car. This is normal. Sometimes they will also need proof of insurance.

Don't discuss financing or let the salesperson know whether you're trading in a car. With both, say you haven't decided yet; keeping your options open. Remember, the test drive comes **WAY** before any negotiations on price. After the test drive, you might feel ready to wheel and deal, **don't**! You won't know what you've missed unless you test drive some more cars.

Talking with your salesperson you'll get a feeling for the dealership's personality and will quickly find out if you need to go elsewhere. Your peace of mind is a crucial element in the car buying process. Are these people helping you to make a smart car selection? Remember you can always leave and go to another dealer if you feel uncomfortable or feel you're being mistreated. Be sure you get a thorough demonstration of each car you are considering.

Chapter 5 *Negotiating the Deal, Step by Step*

Alright you have prepared yourself by doing all the research necessary for this car buying experience and you have chosen which car or cars will suit your needs and maybe even some of your wants. You have used affordability calculators at Edmunds.com to see what price ranges you should be in. Finally you have received, checked and disputed any and all discrepancies on your credit report and have ordered new follow up reports from the 3 major credit bureaus to ensure their accuracy. Now you have everything you need so that you can enter the dealerships with the confidence of a seasoned negotiator. Let's illustrate some key points to remember between your advantages as an educated buyer.

- Without you; the customer, there is no deal to be negotiated in any dealership or used car lot anywhere.

- You are going to pick the time and place of your purchase, the dealership can't, they can only hope.

- You can offer up any information to the salesperson that you want or you can remain quiet and reserved and offer up no intentions. Some key points to this is to **not** offer up a monthly payment desired or the down payment amount you are prepared to pay. Your main concern whether buying or leasing is the total sales price of the car.

- Your price that you are willing to pay for this car should only be known to you until you've exhausted all honest negotiations. Then you may offer this number to them and ask them to call you if they can honor this deal within a reasonable amount of time. Then smile politely and leave.

- The most important negotiating tool you have is to leave at anytime during negotiations. Don't become irritated and leave. Just thank them for their time and leave politely. If it becomes an argument they will likely stand their ground or even recant any and all offers. That will no longer be a place to negotiate with anymore.

- Don't get discouraged and start to think that you're not going to be able to buy or lease this car at the right price. This process could take weeks or maybe even months. Sooner or later a salesperson is going to reconnect with you in hopes of closing a sale.

Be realistic about your expectations of this process if you are serious about making this deal you will be taken seriously. Don't expect the dealership or used car lot to negotiate in a deal that is below their cost. Nobody goes into business, hires all those people and expects to lose money on a deal. Be serious and fair in your negotiations and you should be able to get the best possible prices from the dealership.

So let's get started and negotiate for your next new or used car purchase or lease. You'll visit the dealerships that carry the car or cars that you're interested in or the used car lots in your areas that seem to have the types of cars you prefer. You'll go back to your internet sources to get the current incentives, rebates and/or end of year clearance information. You will take all of that information and check your financing calculators to see what fits in your budget. You will check your banking references and pre-approval amounts and terms available to you. Enter all of the important facts and figures into a notebook so you will have handy references immediately **after** visiting each individual dealer. Do not bring your notebook into the dealership with you.

You have gone shopping for the car or cars on your list and you know there are manufacturer to dealer incentives available to purchase and similar incentives to lease. You will apply these incentives to your target negotiation prices and see if the dealerships will honor or negotiate towards these numbers.

Now you can choose between buying and leasing your car. Until this point it may or may not have made sense to determine lease versus buy because some of the manufacturer to dealer incentives do not apply to leasing a car and you have chosen to negotiate the best possible price of your car, not the best lease payment or monthly loan payment. So how are you going to determine what is best for you? Simple, your budget amount will be put against your needs. If your needs now and in the near future is to have a dependable car, but your budget is not allowing a full purchase payment, then lease the car and save for the time when the lease matures. You can re-assess your financial situation at any time. Most leases are for 2 – 3 years. This way you are only paying for your use. If your financial situation changes than you may purchase at lease end. On the other hand if your budget allows for any car that's in your needs category and then some, then by all means purchase the car. You can probably negotiate with your bank easier and with greater savings than you can with the dealerships preferred financial institution, whereas a lease is commonly best when written by the manufacturer's financial arm.

Leasing began as an economical way to provide vehicles for business use. Their expense was able to be deducted for the operation of business. Today leasing provides an individual to drive more car than what could otherwise be unaffordable. If you are a small business owner or use your vehicle exclusively for business, leasing may be a good idea. Dealers will tell you that a lease is good for people who want to drive a new car all the time. Leasing also appeals when people want lower monthly payments. You have all the responsibilities of ownership with none of its advantages. Or you can look at it this way; you have all the responsibilities of ownership but are not tied to the same vehicle past the lease maturity date. Leases limit the number of miles you can drive. If you drive over your allowed mileage, you will pay the finance company, usually $.15 per mile over your total allowed mileage. A benefit to leasing is also in tax savings. Most state sales tax will be for the value of payments to be made. Since this is only a percentage of the cars value you will pay tax on a smaller percentage of the vehicles price, usually about half the purchase price multiplied by your state sales tax rate. See your tax professional; for further details of this savings. If you buy the car, sales tax is due all at once. It may be able to be part of the financing package. When you lease a vehicle residual value is the amount it will be worth at the end of the lease. Depreciation is the difference between the selling price and the residual value estimated by the leasing company, expressed as a percentage of MSRP. If the car is in high demand it will have a higher than average residual value. Before you lease, check out the residual values of the cars you're considering at the Edmunds or Kelley Bluebook websites.

Your trade, if any should not be discussed until you are satisfied that the sales price of the car is at rock bottom and the dealer can do no better. Your trade can be artificially accounted for in favor of its true value to entice you the buyer into signing a contract that represents more than you expected for your trade. For example, the MSRP of a car you're interested in is $30,000.00 and a factory to dealer incentive is available to you for $2,500.00 cash back by taking delivery by January 31, 20XX So the deal to you is $27,500.00 minus your trade of $5,000 Total price is now $22,500.00. Okay sounds good, but you just paid MSRP for the car and didn't even realize because of the trade and dealer incentives that clouded up the deal. You were probably very pleased to get $5,000.00 for the car you estimated to be at $3,000.00. So you probably could have saved and additional $2,000.00 off of MSRP.

Now let's look at this deal from an educated buyer's point of view. MSRP $30,000.00 Invoice is 26,500.00 factory to dealer incentive nationally advertised $2,500.00 and your true trade in value for your car is $3,000.00. Your target should be $21,000.00 total sales price, of which you agree to put 20% down and finance the remainder and taxes and fees through the dealer's financial institution. Even if you appear to have been given a deal at cost there are still 3 sources of income to the dealer on this deal. The overage in interest rate, is an income source, the sales price of the trade (remember the trade in value is what the dealer might pay for it, but after advertising it and having to warranty it, they can sell it now for $5,500 or so). And finally dealer holdback from the manufacturer, usually 2%-3% of dealer invoice, this is not usually money that's normally negotiable. It is a private agreement between the dealers and the manufacturers and helps to offset the costs of doing business selling and inventorying the manufacturer's products.

Back in Chapter 1 Getting Started with Your Purchase, we talked about the dealers preferred financial institutions and how the dealership is able to quote rates higher than the actual rate charged for the financing. So be very aware that the dealer may artificially react to your credit inquiries in similar fashion and may predict your rate to be high based on whatever factors you give them about your credit worthiness. So just a note… Do not discuss your credit history at all if you intend to finance the car through the dealership. In this instance you will not be offering any information about your credit, only vague statements, (I don't know, Excellent, etc.). Your research should already tell you your credit score and you cannot be misled by someone's deflated score predictions to weaken your financial position in a financed transaction. Commitments from other banks will prove to be very valuable during these negotiations because another source of income may be walking out the door if they can't offer you terms and rates that are comparable to your other offers.

The best time to buy a car is when you're ready to buy. However, dealerships track their sales on a monthly basis, so purchasing at the very end of the month may get you a better deal. Most advertising discounts will always be available, with the exception of year-end model closeouts, which can be a good deal.

Your salesperson may claim every new offer and counteroffer must be approved by a manager. Sometimes they really do have to run offers by a manager, sometimes not. But, either way, you're left sitting alone for long periods of time. Tell the salesperson you want to talk with the manager directly, within a certain amount of time and be prepared to leave by then if you're still waiting.

Salespeople usually start talking price by discussing monthly payments. For example, "If I could get you this car for $290 a month, would you be able to take it today?" Do not let them continue with their monthly payment plan. Politely tell them you're only interested in establishing the dealer's selling price. Make it clear you're seriously interested in buying a car if you can settle on a price that's fair for everyone. If your salesperson can't tell you the dealer's invoice and asking price go to another dealer.

Try to negotiate up from invoice price, not down from sticker price. MSRP is a suggested retail price that is put in place by the manufacturer, unless you're looking for a vehicle in short supply, don't pay MSRP. You're aware of the 2% to 3% holdback the dealer will receive from the manufacturer when the vehicle is sold. High volume dealerships qualify for additional manufacturer discounts, making them more willing to sell vehicles near invoice. If you negotiate up from dealer invoice the actual price negotiations shouldn't take long. Don't offer higher bids unless the dealer reciprocates with lower prices and keep your price increases under $100 per offer. Know your target price, and be prepared to walk if you come to an impasse.

Chapter 6 *Trading in Your Old Car*

Now it's time to consider what you're going to do with your old car. You have 3 options for the most part. You can donate your car to a charity and take a tax deduction (consult your tax advisor) or you can sell it privately using print advertisement and/or signs on the vehicle. You can also trade it in at the dealer that is selling you your new car. Be fair and use Kbb.com wholesale value for this negotiation. They usually have to prepare your old car for sale and in most cases have to offer at least a 30 day warranty on this car, these costs are reflected in the wholesale pricing found on Kbb.com. So try to come as close to this number as possible and don't accept vague numbers or, "We'll see what the used car manager say's next week."

We discussed not revealing your intentions of your trade because this can hide an amount of value in the overall deal. Your trade should not affect the sales price of the car you're buying. The sale of the new car is separate from the trade of the used car. If the dealer doesn't see it this way they are most likely going to fluff up your trade price to make the deal look more attractive, while the difference could have been in the new car price. The value of factory incentives, rebates or low APR financing can easily be erased if your trade enters the picture too early.

You need to make sure your trade in looks as good as it can by having it cleaned up by a detailer, shined and possibly some of the scratches removed. You also want to clear out any of the clutter inside and don't leave any indications in the car or trunk that suggest you have problems with it. (Ex: jumper cables, extra quarts of oil, etc.) All this will increase its value so the appraiser can get a good idea of what the car is worth on his/her used car lot. Minor repairs may be necessary, but don't get involved in any major repairs. Save your money for your new vehicle.

When taking in a trade, the used-car manager assesses the condition, age, and mileage of the vehicle to estimate how much the car would bring at a wholesale auction or how much it should sell for on his lot. If the car is in poor condition and not of the same quality as his current inventory he/she may immediately decide to wholesale it for a quick sale. Again none of this should affect the new car price. If the price they offer you is way below its value, it's likely they don't want any part of your trade because they feel it will not be profitable for them. At this point you may want to sell it privately; usually a private sale will bring you more money. Obviously this will take longer. Maybe tell your salesperson you'll be back after you sell it privately. That may increase the value of the trade all by itself.

Keep in mind the sales tax benefit of the value of your trade. Most states collect sales tax only on the difference in cost between the trade-in value and the price of the new car. This savings might help between the difference of retail value and wholesale value. Do your calculations as part of affordability exercises and keep these figures in your notes so you can refer back to them. This benefit may not be available to you if the sales tax is being calculated by the selling dealer. Be prepared when the numbers are presented to you. In addition, there are no advertisements to pay for, no phone calls or messages to deal with, test drives or potential lawsuits to deal with. Once the car is given to the dealer and the paperwork is signed it becomes their property.

If you're going to sell it privately put a "For Sale" sign in the window and list it locally in your local newspaper's classified section. Anyone looking for a car will start their search there. Include the year; make and model, if it has low mileage include that in your ad (LOW MILES or 20K MILES). If it has high mileage don't list that at all. Mention the number of cylinders in the engine (4, 6, or 8) and whether it has a standard or automatic transmission (STD, AUTO). Keep the ad short and sweet, but don't forget to mention four wheel drive (4WD), air-conditioning (AC), CD-players (CD), leather interior (LTHR), and power accessories (LOADED). Always end the advertisement with some complimentary wording like, "IN EXCELLENT

CONDITION." If that tag line is missing, you may not get any calls.

Now you want to check Edmunds or Kelly Blue Book to determine your vehicle's fair market value. Fair market value is somewhere between trade-in and retail. Check dealer ads and classified listings to make sure your asking price is reasonable for your market. If you're happy with that amount put it at the bottom of your ad. Don't forget to include a first name and your phone number.

Other means of advertising can be found at your local convenience stores. Bi-weekly tabloids have classified listings; some of them are set up to be paid upon the sale of the car and are calculated as a percentage of the sale, even if you found your buyer through another source.

Prepare for scheduling hassles when multiple buyers want to see the car at the same time. Prepare for negotiating. Make sure to have a firm idea of how low a price you'll accept. How will you handle competing offers? It seems to be good practice not to accept a down payment because this will tie up the vehicle until that person comes back with the remainder of the sales price. A good rule of thumb is that, "The car is for sale at all times until it is paid for in full, no deposits please." Be prepared for offers significantly lower than your asking price. Always have an absolute rock bottom price in mind, as most classified ad shoppers are looking for a good deal. If you're not getting any calls your asking price may be too high. Lower your asking price if the vehicle is not selling. Unless the car is highly desirable, it may take weeks to sell.

Serious customers will generally want to take a test drive, so keep the car registered and insured. Make sure their license is current, write down their phone number and make a note of any change of address. If you don't accompany them on the road test, try to get a copy of their driver's license and auto insurance card. Make sure they leave you their car keys and ask for an itinerary of their test drive. Refuse test drives to people who show up at your house with no transportation or to anyone who can't meet you at your home or place of business. The recovery rate for stolen cars is poor, and most recovered thefts are badly damaged.

When you find a private cash buyer, the final steps are to transfer the title and fill out the Department of Motor Vehicle's bill of sale. (Required in most states for tax purposes.) Photocopy the signed transfer papers and keep them on file in case the buyer gets in an accident on their way home. Don't forget to cancel your insurance and turn in your plates.

If your going to donate your car for a tax deduction make sure you and your tax professional are aware of qualified receivers of donated cars. There are a lot of recyclers that are willing to take your old car for its scrap value and usually will not qualify as a donation to a charity. The recyclers have found increased value in some key parts of cars, for instance; the catalytic converter(s) contain rhodium and platinum, both very expensive precious metals. Aluminum parts are also being manufactured more and more into today's cars. So be careful who gets your car for a charitable cause.

The advantages of a potential tax deduction and the satisfaction of giving valuable resources to the charity of your choice are reasons for considering a charitable donation. You will need to determine your vehicle's fair market value. Use IRS publication 561 "Determining the Value of Donated Property." A definition of fair market value is as follows, "Fair market value is the price at which property would change hands between a willing buyer and a willing seller, neither being required to buy or sell, and both having reasonable knowledge of all relevant facts." Most Churches, Synagogues, Temples, Mosques and other religious organizations qualify for charitable donations.

The receiving group gives you a letter or receipt describing the gift, its VIN#, year, make and model. You are responsible for determining the fair market value, not the charity. The IRS forbids charity-assigned values as a conflict of interest. If the car is valued over $5,000.00, you may need to get an independent appraisal (also deductible) to file with your tax documents. Be certain to discuss with your tax professional all the benefits of donating valuable property to charity.

Chapter 7 *Final Negotiations*

If you have enough cash on hand for your down payment (20%), the special (1.9% example) financing could save you money over the life of your loan. When financing your car you want your rebates and incentives applied as part of the down payment. You may also want your trade, if any, applied as a cash down payment. Remember you probably already own your trade so it's as good as cash and has already been taxed.

A deal with a rebate should be written as follows: The dealership adds up the negotiated purchase price, applicable taxes, license fees, document fees, etc. into a grand total. Then your down payment, including the rebate and any cash you submit is subtracted from that total. The resulting balance will be your final price. (The amount due at delivery or amount to be financed)

Negotiating for a used car is the same as new vehicle negotiations, except that there's no dealer invoice. Just a dealers cost of acquiring the car and preparing it for sale as well as any finance charges for being financed on the lot. Although dealers itemize every expense preparing a used vehicle, they don't show you that worksheet. Franchised dealers make their biggest profits from used vehicles. On the plus side, they usually have the cleanest, lowest mileage used cars and often offer factory certified used vehicles. Smaller, non-franchised, specialist dealers don't make nearly as much profit, but their expenses and overhead are significantly less. Their warranties are not generally as good, and they may not have repair facilities.

Successful negotiating of a used car depends on you knowing the fair market value of the vehicle you're interested in. By this point you should have had it inspected by your mechanic, who has provided you with a comprehensive list of repairs that may need to be done to bring the car to a fair market value. You are at a slight disadvantage here because the dealer knows your mechanic has approved the purchase; but you will be prepared to leave if they are unwilling to negotiate. Knowing what fair market value is, you could offer 85%, and stop at 90% or you could start with subtracting 100% of the repair cost from the asking price and haggle up to 50% of the difference of the two prices. (The price difference between the asking price minus repair estimate and the fair market value minus the repair estimate)

Show the dealer your mechanic's estimate. If you're buying a car with an asking price of $8,000 dollars (with a fair market value of $7,400) and your repair estimate is for $1,200, we suggest offering the dealer $6,200 to start with. Don't offer more money unless the dealer comes down an according amount. Keep your increments to no more than $100 a shot. If you don't have an agreement when you reach your limit, leave politely and ask them to, "call you soon if we can come to an agreement."

After you've negotiated a price for your vehicle, most salespeople will escort you to the dealer's business office to sign your final sale or leasing contract. Be sure your negotiated prices for the car and trade in, are on the sales contract and approved by you and the dealer indicated by signatures in most instances. At smaller dealers, the sales manager handles this job as well. Here is where you need to be alert to everything being said and certain that all negotiations of price and your trade in are present and accurate. Be very wary about interest reductions by purchasing an extended warranty or credit life insurance, but listen to the rates being offered because you are going to insist on those rates without those extra purchases. Remember they can and will quote you a higher rate than that being offered by the financial institutions. Also make sure you are not paying for pre-delivery inspections or sometimes referred to as "destination charges." These are paid to the dealer by the manufacturer. Delivery is mostly found on new cars that the manufacturer puts on the sticker price and that is also negotiable. If it ends up on your contract have it removed. Extended warranty policy we covered earlier on when you will need them and remember they can usually be purchased at a later date from the manufacturer. So determine how long you will have the car and how comprehensive the manufacturer's original warranty is. The last place you want to buy insurance is from an auto dealer, unless you're buying used. Decline the extended warranty for now. If you need an extended warranty, keep in mind that the price of coverage is negotiable. Aftermarket installations of remote starters and alarm systems can wreak havoc on your car electrical and electronic systems so be aware of what warranties are included with these items and how to obtain warranty service.

Make sure your contract of sale does not have a "subject to financing clause." You want to make certain that you are approved for the terms and conditions that were set forth to you in the truth in lending clause or "cost of financing" document. If anything in the contract appears to be missing or out of line, tell them before you sign. You need everything clarified satisfactorily to you, especially claims of higher interest rate because of the lack of an extended warranty policy or credit life insurance.

Finally use the time necessary to read the contract completely. After you sign, it doesn't matter what the finance manager says, if you signed it, you also agreed to it and if it's wrong, it's usually too late. If your figures to buy your car were $488.00 per month and their figure is $509.00. Something was added in and needs to be questioned and scrutinized before signing. $21.00 per month for 48 months is $1,008.00. Not a bad sum to be overlooked.

If anything goes wrong in the finance office you should be able to walk away at anytime or you can present a check from your financial institution for the due on delivery amount that you have negotiated with the salesperson, this will eliminate the finance office completely.

Chapter 8 *The Delivery Process*

This is the final step in the new car buying process. Supply the dealer with the right paperwork and make sure the car is delivered to you exactly as agreed on during the negotiations.

It's a good idea to look the car over completely and resolve any issues that are unsatisfactory. You want to operate the car to be sure everything is working as designed and any questions you have about its operation and maintenance are answered completely to your satisfaction. Remember you're not buying a loaf of bread this is a substantial purchase and should not be taken lightly or with too much humor. If you're not satisfied now, how do you think you will feel halfway through your loan obligation? Be very careful that this is the car you bargained for and does not appear to have been damaged in any way.

If you're buying from a dealer, go over your vehicle carefully before you accept it. Many manufacturers have a delivery checklist that your salesperson must review with you before handing over the keys. Check for a jack and spare tire, an owner's manual in the glove box, and see that any accessories that you specified in your contract have been done. Look at the odometer to make sure the "new" car you're buying isn't actually a demonstrator. New vehicles usually won't have more than 100 miles on their odometer, unless it was obtained in a dealer to dealer trade. Double-check your financing agreement before you sign it. If you're buying, make sure the agreement is a loan contract, and if you're leasing, a lease contract. Make sure the numbers are what you agreed to. Once you've signed the papers and accepted your vehicle, the car is yours.

If the amounts shown on any documents are higher than you agreed to or if your interest rate went up 2% overnight, get an explanation. If the original figures don't re-appear, politely ask for your deposit back and be ready to leave. Usually the dealer will back down and apologize for the mistake. They might leave you there for 20 or 30 minutes, hoping you'll tire of the wait and give in.

If you financed through the dealer, don't take delivery of the car until you have the payment book or at least a signed copy of the "cost of borrowing" statement. This statement should include the amount financed, the interest rate, the number of payments and the amount that will be paid over the entire length of the term. Without this document it may not be clear how much the financing is going to cost for this car you're about to leave with. Don't let them put you in this situation. Refuse delivery until the payment book arrives and your original financing transaction is complete.

To get new plates or transfer your existing plates, you must present proof of insurance to the selling dealer or your state's Department of Motor Vehicles (DMV). Your insurance agent will give you or fax to the selling dealer, a new insurance identification card, listing your carrier, policy number, VIN# (vehicle identification number), and your name and address. Make sure the VIN# is correct and that the address on the card matches your driver's license exactly. If you're transferring plates, your current vehicle's registration will also be needed. If you're buying from a private party you will also need to give the DMV a bill of sale signed by the seller.

Most car dealers will register your car as part of the service they perform for a fee. Most DMV offices are busy and the process can be complicated and time consuming. Some states allow larger dealers to operate DMV satellite offices right in the dealership. The forms required vary from state to state, so if the dealer isn't doing it for you, call the local DMV office to find out ahead of time what you'll need to bring.

You should by now be very pleased with yourself having gone through all of the necessary steps to insure you got the best price and terms possible while purchasing the car that fits your needs best.

Compare some of the steps you've taken during this purchase and study how you could have perfected them for your next purchase and be confident that you have the ability to negotiate your next vehicle purchase/lease.

Glossary of Purchase Terms

APR
The "Annual Percentage Rate" is a yearly rate of interest that includes fees and costs paid to acquire the loan. Lenders are required by law to disclose the APR, and the rate is used to compare various loans available, making even simple interest and compound interest loans comparable.

Absolute Low (floor price)
The lowest price a seller is willing to take for a vehicle.

Acceleration Clause
This allows a lender to speed up a loan rate if there is a default on the loan.

Accessories
The added features that are available for a new car.

Accrued Interest
Interest that increases on an unpaid balance of a loan.

Advertising Fee
The car dealer will pass this fee on to the buyer for advertising costs.

Agreement of Sale
Also referred to as sales or purchase agreement. It states that the seller is selling and the buyer is buying.

Amortization
Payment of a loan obligation in a series of installments or transfers.

Application
An initial statement of personal and financial information required to approve your loan.
Appraisal
An opinion of the market value of an asset as of a specific date.
Appraisal Fee
The fee to estimate any property or possession.
Asset
Tangible items (possessions or property) to secure a debt.
Assignment
Any transfer of your loan from one lender to another lender.
Auction
The sale process by which multiple bidders compete to purchase a vehicle that is finally sold to the individual offering the highest price.
Balloon Note
At the end of the loan term, some of or the entire original loan amount is due and payable.
Bankruptcy
A debtor that, upon voluntary petition or one invoked by the debtor's creditors is judged legally insolvent. The debtor's remaining property is then administered for the creditors or is distributed among them.
Base Price
The cost of a car without options, but including standard equipment, factory warranty, and freight. This price is printed on the Monroney sticker.

Bid
The amount of money offered for a vehicle in the sale.
Billing Error
The Federal Fair Credit Billing Act defines this as any mistake on your statement.
Bill of Sale
A document provided by a seller showing the name of the purchaser and purchase price, which is also used to calculate sales and other taxes.
Black Book
A bi weekly guidebook on used car prices that summarizes the most recent wholesale prices directly from auctions. Values often are "extra clean, clean, average or rough"; adjustments can be made for mileage, trim level, and optional equipment.
Borrowing
To obtain or receive something on loan with the promise or understanding of returning it or its equivalent.
Broker
Someone who helps negotiates or arranges but does not make the loan.
Business Days
Holidays and weekends are not usually considered a business day.
Buyers Guide
The Federal Trade Commission requires auto dealers to show a Buyers Guide for each used car they sell.
Buyers Order
The contract between a buyer and seller.

Buy-Here, Pay-Here (BHPH)
Dealer-provided financing to customers who are unable to obtain credit. BHPH dealers sell mechanically sound, affordable vehicles for which customers generally return to the dealership weekly or monthly to pay off the dealer-provided credit for their car.
Captive Finance Company
A leasing or finance company that is associated with a vehicle manufacturer.
Certificate of Origin
A document that conveys the title of vehicle from the manufacturer to the dealer.
Certificate of Title
A legal document issued by the state showing the owner's name and the vehicle's mileage at the time of sale.
Closed-End Lease
A lease in which the lessee is not responsible for any difference between the actual and estimated residual value at the time of lease maturity. The lessee's only extra obligations under a closed-end lease might be mileage or wear and tear exceeding the lease contract provisions.
Cloud On Title
A claim that negatively affects an outstanding title.
Co-Buyer
A Co-Buyer's (Spouse) income is counted toward the buyer's income.

Collateral
Property or possessions used to support a loan that in default of your loan payment can be seized.
Collision Insurance
In the event of damage to your car this insurance pays for repairs.
Commitment
A legal binding agreement between a lender and a borrower.
Compound Interest
Interest paid on the principal and its accrued interest.
Comprehensive Insurance
This insurance covers damages from theft, vandalism or other natural causes (weather).
Co-Signer
This person assumes equal responsibility for the loan if the borrower does not pay.
Credit
Reputation for solvency and integrity entitling a person to be trusted in buying or borrowing.
Creditor
A lender who is owed money.
Creditworthiness
The ability to repay loans or debts in the past or future.
Credit Bureau
A firm that provides credit and personal information to creditors.
Credit History
A document that shows borrowing and repayment of debts.

Credit Profile
The report showing your history of money borrowed and other financial obligations.
Credit Report
A credit document that shows credit or loan account, balances, employment and financial transactions.
Credit Scoring
Banks and lending institutions use different scoring systems to decide your creditworthiness.
Dealer
An individual licensed by the state to conduct the sale and purchase of new or used vehicles.
Dealer Charges
These charges are for options offered by the dealer.
Dealer Incentives
Auto manufacturers offer programs to dealers to increase sales.
Dealer Invoice
The purchase price of the vehicle that the dealer is required to pay the manufacturer.
Dealer Sticker Price
Sticker price or MSRP is the total price of the vehicle.
Debt Ratio
Your earnings compared to how much you owe.
Default
Failure to meet the repayment or other terms of your loan.

Depreciation
The value lost as the vehicle ages. During the early years of the vehicle's life depreciation is usually rapid and can be greater or less than the average because of mileage and wear and tear.
Destination Charge
Shipping charges of the car that is passed on to the buyer.
Disclosure Statement
The total amount of the loan; the loan amount, interest and other financial charges.
Down Payment
The difference between the loan amount and the purchase price; usually paid immediately upon purchase in the form of cash or trade-in value.
Equity
The positive difference between the trade-in or market value of a vehicle and the loan payoff amount, in an installment sale of loan. The equity is the market value of the vehicle when the loan is paid off.
Fair Market Value
The current value of a particular vehicle in the marketplace, based on mileage, exterior and interior condition, mechanical fitness, etc.
Financing
The management of money, banking, investments, and credit.
Franchised Dealer
A licensed vehicle dealer authorized to sell and service a specific brand of new vehicles.

Gross Income
For qualifying purposes, the income of the borrower before taxes or expenses are deducted.
Incentives
A form of reward offered to boost sales; a special price reduction or rebate from vehicle manufacturers to influence the sale of a particular model. Incentives can be low to zero percent.
Independent Dealer
A used vehicle dealer who is not associated with a manufacturer.
Insurance
Coverage by a contract binding a party to indemnify another against specified loss in return for premiums paid.
Interest
A charge for a loan, usually a percentage of the amount loaned.
Interest Rate
The percentage of a sum of money charged for its use.
Kelley Blue Book
A publication that lists retail prices and retail trade-in values of used vehicles.
Lending
To provide money temporarily on condition that the amount borrowed be returned, usually with an interest fee.
Lease
A contract between a lessor and a lessee for the use of a vehicle or other property, subject to stated terms and limitations, for a specified period and at a specified payment.
Lessee
The company or individual to whom a vehicle is leased.

Lessor
The party to a lease agreement who holds legal or tax title to the vehicle and receives the lease payments.

Lien
The right to take and hold or sell the property of a debtor as security or payment for a debt or duty.

Loan
That which one lends or borrows, especially a sum of money lent at interest.

Lock or Lock In
A commitment obtained from a lender assuring a particular interest rate or feature for a definite time period. Provides protection should interest rates rise between the loan application, loan approval, and closure and receipt of the borrowed funds.

Manufacturer's Rebate
A program offered directly to the buyer by manufacturers to increase the sales of slow-selling models or to reduce excess inventories.

Manufacturer's Suggested Retail Price (MSRP)
The suggested retail price listed on the Monroney label. Also referred to as the "sticker price."

Money Factor
A percentage representing the cost of the money required to lease a vehicle, similar to the interest rate paid on a loan.

Monroney Sticker Price
Required by federal law, the price which appears on a label affixed to the car window showing the base price, the manufacturer's installed options with the manufacturer's suggested retail price, the manufacturer's freight or transportation charge, and the fuel economy (mileage). The label may not be removed by anyone other than the purchaser.

National Independent Automobile Dealers Association (NADA)
Formed in 1946 to represent independent automobile dealers nationwide, the organization provides its 16,000 members with solutions to help them operate businesses that are more successful.

Open-End Lease
A lease where no specific time limit is set for the vehicle to remain in service. In most cases, at the end of the lease, any gain or loss from the sale of the vehicle belongs to the lessee.

Private Transaction
When one consumer sells a vehicle to another consumer without the interaction of a car dealer.

Repossession
To reclaim possession of for failure to pay installments due.

Residual Value
The amount agreed upon to represent the value of the car at the termination of a lease, usually determined by the amount of depreciation in the car's value predicted during the term of the lease.

Retail Price
The price paid by a consumer to a dealer or individual for a vehicle. The dealer or individual sets the retail price of a used car by calculating the wholesale price paid plus reconditioning expenses and other costs.
Term
The length of time that a lessee will make payments on a loan. Typical car loans have terms of 24, 36 or 48 months.
Title
A legal document issued by the state showing the owner's name and the vehicle's mileage at the time of sale.
Trade-in
A vehicle that is sold to either a new or used car dealer as part of the purchase of another.
Trade-in Value
The amount a dealership credits the buyer for the vehicle provided as partial or full payment for another vehicle. Amount credited is frequently about 5% below the wholesale value of the vehicle.
Underwriting
The process of verifying data and approving a loan.
Upfront Costs
Fees and charges collected at the time of the loan, as opposed to over the life of the loan. May reduce the interest rate paid over the life of the loan.
Upside-down
When the value of a vehicle is lower than the outstanding balance of the loan secured by the vehicle.

Used Car Guidebooks
Publications that report current wholesale and/or retail prices of vehicles. Prices are listed according to year, make, model, options, mileage, and condition of the vehicle. Prices are generally determined from factors such as auto auction prices, retail sales prices, other wholesale transactions, and regional demand. Major examples are: Automotive Market Report (AMR), Black Book, Kelley Blue Book, and National Automobile Dealers Association (NADA) official Used Car Guide.

Vendor
One that sells or vends.

Waive
To give up a claim or right voluntarily; relinquish.

Wholesaler
A dealer who buys vehicles at auction – or from a dealer or another wholesaler – and resells them in the wholesale market, i.e., to dealers rather than consumers. Wholesalers also buy and sell cars among the dealers with whom they do business.

Yield
The annual rate of return on an investment, expressed as a percentage.

Glossary of Lease Terms

Acquisition fee

A charge included in most lease transactions that either is paid up front or is included in the gross capitalized cost; may be called a bank fee, an administrative fee or an assignment fee. This fee usually covers a variety of administrative or insurance costs. These may include the costs of obtaining a credit report, verifying insurance coverage, checking the accuracy and completeness of the lease documentation, entering the lease in data processing and accounting systems and purchasing insurance for or reserving funds for residual-value losses, gap-coverage losses and other lease losses. Without an acquisition fee, lessor's have to charge higher rental charges.

Actuarial method

See Constant Yield method.

Additional insured

A party that is covered by another party's insurance policy. The lessor typically requires you to name the lessor or assignee as an additional insured under your vehicle insurance policy.

Adjusted capitalized cost (adjusted cap cost)

The amount capitalized at the beginning of the lease, equal to the gross capitalized cost minus the capitalized cost reduction. This amount is sometimes referred to as the net cap cost.

Amortized amounts
Amounts such as taxes, fees, charges for service contracts, payments for insurance and any prior credit or lease balance that are included in the gross capitalized cost and are paid as part of the base monthly payment.

Amount due at lease signing or delivery
The total of any capitalized cost reduction, monthly payments paid at signing, security deposit, title and registration fees and other amounts due before you take delivery of the vehicle.

APR (annual percentage rate)
The annualized cost of credit expressed as a percentage; used in finance agreements. An annual percentage rate, or an equivalent rate, is not used in leasing agreements.

Arranger
See Broker.

Assignee
A third party that buys a lease agreement from a lessor. You become obligated to the assignee, and the assignee generally assumes the responsibilities of the lessor.

Assignment
The sale of a lease agreement and transfer of the ownership rights for the leased vehicle from the lessor to an assignee. Many leases are assigned at the time the lease is signed.

Assignor
A lessor that sells the lease agreement and transfers the ownership rights for the leased vehicle to an assignee.

Base monthly payment
The portion of the monthly payment that covers depreciation, any amortized amounts and rent charges; calculated by adding the amount of depreciation, any other amortized amounts and rent charges and dividing the total by the number of months in the lease. Monthly sales/use taxes and other monthly fees are added to this base monthly payment to determine the total monthly payment.

Broker (or Arranger)
An entity that arranges for the sale or lease of vehicles through another party.

Business lease
A lease of personal property to (1) an individual to be used primarily for business, commercial or agricultural purposes or (2) an organization, such as a partnership, corporation or government agency

Capitalized cost
Shortened term for either gross capitalized cost or adjusted capitalized cost. Disclosure of both types of costs is required under federal law. Some states require that the term "capitalized cost" be used in state lease disclosures. *See* Gross capitalized cost *and* Adjusted capitalized cost.

Capitalized cost reduction (cap cost reduction)
The sum of any down payment, net trade-in allowance and rebate used to reduce the gross capitalized cost. The cap cost reduction is subtracted from the gross cap cost to get the adjusted cap cost.

Captive finance company
　A finance company related to a particular automobile manufacturer or distributor.

Closed-end lease (or Walk-away lease)
　A lease in which you are not responsible for the difference if the actual value of the vehicle at the scheduled end of the lease is less than the residual value (though you may be responsible for excessive wear and excess mileage charges and for other lease requirements). *Distinguish from* Open-end lease.

Consumer lease
　A lease of personal property to an individual to be used primarily for personal, family or household purposes for a period of more than 4 months and with a total contractual obligation of no more than $25,000. A lease meeting all these criteria is covered by the Consumer Leasing Act and Federal Reserve Board Regulation M. If any one of these criteria is not met, for example, if the leased property is used primarily for business purposes or if the total contractual obligation exceeds $25,000, the Consumer Leasing Act and Regulation M do not apply. *See* Total contractual obligation.

Consumer Leasing Act
　A 1976 amendment to the federal Truth in Lending Act that requires disclosure of the cost and terms of consumer leases and also places substantive restrictions on consumer leases. *See* Consumer lease.

Consummation
　Generally, the time at which you and the lessor sign the lease agreement.

Dealer preparation fee
A fee charged by some dealers to cover the expenses of preparing a vehicle for lease. The dealer may be reimbursed by the manufacturer for this expense.

Default
Your failure to meet one or more conditions of your lease agreement. Default may result in early termination of the lease.

Depreciation and any amortized amounts
Total of (1) amount charged to cover the vehicle's projected decline in value through normal use during the lease term and (2) other items that are paid for over the lease term; calculated as the difference between the adjusted capitalized cost and the vehicle's residual value. This amount is a major part of your base monthly payment.

Disclosures
Information on the financial terms and other terms and conditions of a lease, including information required by federal regulation (Regulation M) and by state laws. Required disclosures must be made in writing before the lease is consummated. Advertisements that include key lease terms (the amount of any payment or a statement of payments due before consummation or delivery) must also include certain disclosures. Under Regulation M, certain disclosures must be grouped together and segregated from other information (*see* Segregated disclosures). Other required disclosures must appear elsewhere in the lease documents (*see* Nonsegregated disclosures).

Disposition fee (disposal fee)
A fee often charged by a lessor or assignee to defray the cost of preparing and selling the vehicle at the end of the lease if you do not purchase the vehicle but instead return it to the lessor or assignee.

Documentation fee
A fee charged by some dealerships (who may call it a dealer documentation fee) or other lessor's to cover the cost of preparing lease documents.

Down payment
An initial cash payment in a lease that reduces the capitalized cost or is applied to other amounts due at lease signing. *See* Capitalized cost reduction.

Early termination
Ending of the lease before the scheduled termination date for any reason, voluntary or involuntary (for example, you return the vehicle early or default on the lease, or the vehicle is stolen or totaled). In most cases of early termination, you must pay an early termination charge.

Early termination charge
The amount you owe if your lease ends before its scheduled termination date, calculated as described in your lease agreement. The earlier your lease is terminated, the greater this charge is likely to be. The charge is generally the difference between the early termination payoff and the amount credited to you for the vehicle. Suppose, for example, that your early termination payoff amount is $16,000 and the amount credited for the vehicle is $14,000. The early termination charge would be $16,000 minus $14,000, or $2,000.

Early termination payoff (early termination balance or gross payoff)
The total amount you owe if your lease is terminated before the scheduled end of the term, before the value credited to you for the vehicle is subtracted. The early termination payoff is calculated as described in your lease agreement. It may include the unpaid lease balance and other charges.

Equal Credit Opportunity Act
A federal law that prohibits discrimination in credit transactions on the basis of race, color, religion, national origin, sex, marital status, age, source of income or the exercise of any right under the Consumer Credit Protection Act.

Equity
In an installment sale or loan, the positive difference between the trade-in or market value of your vehicle and the loan payoff amount. When the loan is paid off, the equity is the market value of the vehicle.

Excess mileage charge
   A charge by the lessor or assignee for miles driven in excess of the maximum specified in the lease agreement. The excess mileage charge is usually between $0.10 and $0.25 per mile. Suppose, for example, that your lease specifies a maximum of 36,000 miles and a charge of $0.15 per mile over the maximum. If you drive 37,000 miles, the excess mileage charge will be $0.15 x 1,000, or $150. Open-end leases typically do not include an excess mileage charge.

Excessive wear-and-tear charge
   Amount charged by a lessor or assignee to cover wear and tear on a leased vehicle beyond what is considered normal. The charge may cover both interior and exterior damage, such as upholstery stains, body dents and scrapes and tire wear beyond the limits stated in the lease agreement. Open-end leases typically do not include an excessive wear and use charge.

Excessive wear-and-tear coverage
   A plan you may purchase that covers some or all of the charges for excessive wear and tear defined in the lease agreement. The coverage of these plans varies in the amounts and types of charges covered. Most plans deny coverage if the lease is terminated early or if you are in default. Generally, these plans do not cover excess mileage.

Excessive wear-and-use charge
   Sum of the excess mileage charge and the excessive wear-and-tear charge.

Extended warranty
See Service contract.
Fair market value
The amount that a willing buyer would pay to a willing seller to purchase certain property at a particular point in time.
Fair-market-value purchase option
Your right to purchase a leased vehicle at scheduled termination in accordance with the terms specified in your lease agreement for a price determined by referring to a readily available guide to used-car values or another independent source.
Federal Reserve Board
The federal agency with rule-writing authority for the Truth in Lending Act, of which the Consumer Leasing Act is part; officially known as the Board of Governors of the Federal Reserve System. The Board also performs other functions related to U.S. monetary policy, financial system stability, bank supervision and regulation and the nation's payments system.

Federal Trade Commission
The federal agency responsible for enforcing the Truth in Lending Act, of which the Consumer Leasing Act is part, among leasing companies, finance companies, lessor's, and assignees not regulated by other federal agencies. The Federal Trade Commission also performs other functions related to its role of ensuring that the nation's markets function competitively; enforcing other statutes affecting consumer financial services; and enforcing the Federal Trade Commission Act, which prohibits unfair or deceptive acts or practices.

Fees and taxes (or official fees and taxes)
The total amount you will pay for taxes, licenses, registration fees, title fees, and official (governmental) fees over the term of your lease. Because fees and taxes may change during the term of your lease, they may be stated as estimates.

Fixed-price purchase option
Your right to purchase a leased vehicle at scheduled termination for a fixed price specified in your lease agreement.

Full-maintenance lease
A lease in which the lessor or assignee assumes responsibility for all manufacturer-recommended maintenance and service on the vehicle. The lease may also cover additional mechanical repairs and servicing during the term of the lease. The cost of this service usually is included in the gross capitalized cost or is added to the base monthly payment.

Gap amount
In the event a leased vehicle is stolen or totaled, the difference between the early termination payoff amount, not including any past-due amounts, and the amount for which the vehicle is insured before the insurance deductible and any other policy deductions are subtracted. The definition of gap amount may vary in different states or in different lease agreements.

Gap coverage (guaranteed auto protection, or GAP)
A plan that provides you financial protection in case your leased vehicle is stolen or totaled in an accident. Some plans deny gap coverage if you are in default at the time of the loss. There are two types of gap coverage. One is a waiver by the lessor or assignee of the gap amount if the vehicle is stolen or totaled. The other is a contract by a third party to cover the gap amount. Under either type, you may remain responsible for the insurance deductible, for other amounts deducted from the insured amount of the vehicle by your insurance company, and for any past-due or other amounts you owe under the lease. You may also be responsible for the monthly payments until the lessor receives the insurance proceeds.

Gross capitalized cost (gross cap cost)
The agreed-upon value of the vehicle at the time you lease it, which generally may be negotiated, plus any items you agree to pay for over the lease term (amortized amounts), such as taxes, fees, service contracts, insurance, and any prior credit or lease balance.

Incentives
Amounts rebated or credited, or special programs offered to encourage the leasing of certain vehicles.
Independent leasing company
A leasing company that offers leases directly to consumers and businesses and is generally not affiliated with a particular automobile manufacturer.
Insurance
A contract in which one party agrees to pay for another party's financial loss resulting from a specified event (for example, a collision, theft, or storm damage). Lease agreements generally require that you maintain vehicle collision and comprehensive insurance as well as liability insurance for bodily injury and property damage.
Insurance verification
The process of obtaining verbal or written confirmation of required coverage from your insurance agent or company.
Late charge
A fee charged for a past-due payment. This charge is usually either a percentage of the lease payment or a fixed dollar amount.
Late payment
A payment received after the specified due date. In most cases a payment made after any grace period triggers a late charge.
Lease
A contract between a lessor and a lessee for the use of a vehicle or other property, subject to stated terms and limitations, for a specified period and at a specified payment.

Lease balance (adjusted lease balance)
The unpaid portion of the adjusted capitalized cost of the lease. The lease balance is reduced as you make your monthly payments, usually calculated according to a standard method such as the Constant Yield (Actuarial) method. The lease balance is often a primary component of the early termination payoff amount.

Lease charge
See Rent or rent charge.

Lease extension
Continuation of a lease agreement beyond the original term, often 1 month at a time. There may be a charge for extending the lease. If the extension continues beyond 6 months, new lease disclosures must be provided.

Lease factor
See Money factor.

Lease payments
The number of payments in the lease agreement. Generally, the number of payments and the number of months in the lease term are the same. However, there are some leases in which the numbers may be different, such as a single-payment lease, which would disclose "1" as the number of payments and may disclose "24 months" as the lease term.

Lease rate
A percentage used by some lessor's or assignees to describe the rent charge portion of your monthly payment. However, no federal standard exists for calculating the lease rate. Any rates or factors used in lease calculations do not have to be disclosed under federal law. If a lease rate is given as a percentage in an advertisement or on any lease form, the ad or form must also state, "This percentage may not measure the overall cost of financing this lease." Some states may require disclosure of the lease rate calculated according to the state's definition of the lease rate.

Lease term
The period of time for which a lease agreement is written.

Lemon laws
State laws that provide remedies to consumers for vehicles that repeatedly fail to meet certain standards of quality and performance. Lemon laws vary by state and may not cover leased vehicles.

Lessee
The party to whom the vehicle is leased. In a consumer lease, the lessee is you, the consumer. The lessee is required to make payments and to meet other obligations specified in the lease agreement.

Lessor
A person or organization that regularly leases, offers to lease, or arranges for the lease of a vehicle. *See* Assignee and Broker.

Maintenance
Care for the vehicle required by the lease agreement. Maintenance may include manufacturer-recommended servicing and any repairs needed to keep the vehicle in good operating condition.

Maintenance contract
A contract that you may purchase to cover some or all of the vehicle maintenance and servicing. *Distinguish from* Service contract.

Maintenance lease
A lease agreement in which some or all of the vehicle maintenance and servicing is the responsibility of the lessor or assignee.

Mechanical breakdown coverage
See Service contract.

Mileage allowance (or mileage limitation)
The fixed mileage limit for the lease term. If you exceed this limit, you may have to pay an excess mileage charge.

Model lease forms
Sample disclosure forms developed by the Federal Reserve Board. You should receive a similar form before becoming obligated on the lease.

Money factor (or Lease factor)
A number, often given as a decimal, used by some lessor's or assignees to determine the rent charge portion of your monthly payment. This number is not a lease rate and cannot be converted to a lease rate by moving the decimal point.

Monthly payment
This term may refer to one of two required federal disclosures. *See* Base monthly payment and Total monthly payment.

Monthly sales/use taxes
The state and local taxes that you must pay monthly when you lease a vehicle. These payments, if any are added to your base monthly payment and paid as part of your total monthly payment.

MSRP
Manufacturer's suggested retail price, sometimes called the sticker price.

Net capitalized cost
See Adjusted capitalized cost.

Open-end lease
A lease agreement in which the amount you owe at the end of the lease term is based on the difference between the residual value of the leased property and its realized value. Your lease agreement may provide for a refund of any excess if the realized value is greater than the residual value. In an open-end consumer lease, assuming that you have met the mileage and wear standards, the residual value is considered unreasonable if it exceeds the realized value by more than 3 times the base monthly payment (sometimes called the "three-payment rule"). If you believe the amount owed at the end of the lease term is unreasonable and refuse to pay, the lessor or assignee may attempt to prove that the residual value was reasonable when it was set at the beginning of the lease. However, if you cannot reach a settlement with the lessor or assignee, you cannot be

forced to pay the excess amount unless the lessor or assignee brings a successful court action and pays your reasonable attorney's fees. *Distinguish from* Closed-end lease.

Option to purchase
See Purchase option.

Payoff
See Early termination payoff.

Personal property tax (or Ad valorem tax)
A tax on personal property. State laws govern whether personal property taxes apply to a leased vehicle; your lease agreement governs whether you or the lessor or assignee will pay these taxes.

Prior credit balance (negative equity or negative trade-in balance)
The portion of the gross capitalized cost representing the amount due under a previous credit contract after the value of the vehicle traded in on the lease has been credited.

Prior lease balance
The portion of the gross capitalized cost representing the balance due under a previous lease agreement after the value of the previously leased vehicle has been credited.

Purchase option
Your right to buy the vehicle you have leased, before or at the end of the lease term, according to terms specified in the lease agreement. Your lease agreement may or may not include a purchase option.

Purchase-option fee
An amount, in addition to the purchase price, you may have to pay to exercise any purchase option in your lease agreement.

Realized value
(1) The amount received by the lessor or assignee for the leased vehicle at disposition, (2) the highest offer for the lease vehicle at disposition, or (3) the fair market value of the leased vehicle at termination. The realized value may be either the wholesale or the retail value specified in the lease agreement.

Reasonableness standard
The requirement of the Consumer Leasing Act that charges for delinquency, default, or early termination be reasonable in light of the lessor's or assignee's (1) anticipated or actual harm caused by such delinquency, default, or early termination, (2) difficulties in proving loss, and (3) inconvenience in obtaining a remedy.

Rebate
An amount that may be offered by a manufacturer, dealer, lessor, or assignee that may be paid to you separately or credited to your lease agreement.

Reconditioning
The process of preparing a vehicle for resale or re-lease if you return it.

Reconditioning reserve
   An amount you may pay at the beginning of the lease that may be used by the lessor or assignee to offset any amounts you may owe at the end of the lease term for excessive wear and use and excess mileage. Any remaining amount may be refunded to you.

Registration fee
   A fee charged by a state motor vehicle department to register a vehicle and authorize its use on the public roadways.

Rent or rent charge
   The portion of your base monthly payment that is not depreciation or any amortized amounts. This charge is similar to interest on a loan.

Residual value
   The end-of-term value of the vehicle established at the beginning of the lease and used in calculating your base monthly payment. The residual value is deducted from the adjusted capitalized cost to determine the depreciation and any amortized amounts. It is an estimate that may be determined, in part, by using residual value guidebooks. The residual value may be higher or lower than the realized value at the scheduled end of the lease.

Residual value guidebooks
   Publications used, in part, by some lessor's and assignees to establish vehicle residual values. Different guidebooks are more popular in different regions of the United States and with different lessor's and assignees.

Sales/use taxes
   Taxes assessed on leased and purchased vehicles. States differ in which amounts are taxed and when the taxes are assessed. In a lease, sales/use taxes may be assessed on (1) the base monthly payment, (2) any capitalized cost reduction, and (3) in a few states, the adjusted capitalized cost. In most states, the sales/use tax on the base monthly payment is paid monthly; in some states, however, the tax is due at lease inception. Sales/use taxes on the capitalized cost reduction and the adjusted capitalized cost are usually due at lease inception. If you exercise any purchase option, separate taxes may apply.

Security deposit
   An amount you may be required to pay, usually at the beginning of the lease that may be used by the lessor or assignee in the event of default or at the end of the lease to offset any amounts you owe under the lease agreement. Any remaining amount may be refunded to you.

Security interest
   If stated in your lease agreement, a lessor's or assignee's legal right to your property (such as stocks or bonds) that secures payment of your obligation under the lease agreement.

Segregated disclosures
   Disclosures required by Federal Reserve Board Regulation M that must be grouped together and separated from other information in the lease documents. The first page of the sample leasing form shows the disclosures that must be segregated. *See also* Nonsegregated disclosures.

Service contract (or Mechanical breakdown coverage or Extended warranty)
A contract you may purchase to cover such expenses as the repair or replacement of vehicle components and, in some cases, related services such as towing or replacement rental cars. In most cases, service contracts do not cover routine maintenance. *Distinguish from* Maintenance contract.

Single-payment lease
A lease that requires a single payment made in advance rather than periodic payments made over the term of the lease. The single, lump-sum payment should be less than the total amount you would pay if you were to make periodic payments over the term of the lease.

Standards for wear and use
Statements in the lease agreement defining what the lessor or assignee means by normal wear and use and setting the requirements for the vehicle's condition at the end of the lease. Standards may address such items as the minimum amount of tread on the tires at the end of the lease or the type of dents or scratches that are acceptable. These standards must be reasonable.

Sublease
Oral or written contractual transfer of your leased vehicle to another person. Such a transfer is usually prohibited without the lessor's or assignee's approval.

Subvention
A program or plan in which certain items are subsidized by the manufacturer, the finance company, the lessor or the assignee.

Termination fee
See Disposition fee (disposal fee).
Title
Legal document that identifies the owner of the vehicle. The lessor or assignee, not you, holds title to the leased vehicle.
Total contractual obligation
The sum of the capitalized cost reduction, the total of base monthly payments and other charges due under the lease agreement. The total contractual obligation excludes any security deposit as well as sales taxes and any other fees and taxes paid to a third party. If the total contractual obligation exceeds $25,000, the Consumer Leasing Act does not apply.
Total monthly payment
The base monthly payment plus monthly sales or use taxes and any other monthly charges.
Total of payments
The sum of the periodic payments, the end-of-term disposition fee, any other charges and all amounts due at lease signing or delivery, minus refundable amounts such as a security deposit and any monthly payments included in the amount due at lease signing or delivery.
Trade-in
The net value of your vehicle credited toward the purchase or lease of another vehicle.
Use tax
See Monthly sales/use tax.

Used-car guidebooks
Publications that report current wholesale and (or) retail prices of vehicles. Wholesale values generally are determined from such factors as auto auction prices, other wholesale transactions, and regional demand. Prices are listed according to year, make, model, options, mileage and condition of the vehicle. Retail prices are generally determined by such factors as dealership retail sales prices, other retail transactions and regional demand.

Used-vehicle leasing
Leasing of previously driven (owned or leased) vehicles.

Warranty
A guarantee that the vehicle will function and perform as specified. A warranty usually covers specified mechanical problems during a specified period of time or number of miles.

Dealer Slang Terms

$500 sandwich: Went to lunch and missed a sale.

Ad car: A basic car with few options (used to draw customers into the dealership).

Backwards: When a vehicle's wholesale value is less than the amount still owed on the vehicle.

Baldinis: Bald tires.

Be-backs: The customers who tell you not to worry, they'll be back.

Bird dog: Referral fee.

BK: The customer has a bankruptcy in their credit history.

Blow them out: Don't waste any more time with a customer.

Bomb: An old car with no value.

Clip joint: A dealership with a reputation for overcharging.

Crapped out: Deal that didn't materialize.

Cream puff: A used vehicle in excellent condition.

Crop duster: A car that blows smoke out of the tailpipe.

Deadbeat: A customer with a bad credit history.

Dime: $100.

Finn: $500.

Fish: A customer who's too willing to part with their money.

Gasser: A customer who doesn't have the money to buy a vehicle, but acts like they do.

Glass: Obvious use of Bondo or Fiberglas to repair rust or body damage.

Gold Package: Gaudy-looking vehicle.

Gouge: Sell a vehicle for more than sticker price.

Grease: The amount of discount a customer needs to close the deal.

Grease monkey: A mechanic.

Grind: Negotiations that take a long time.

Gross: Amount of profit.

Hammer: Exert pressure on a customer to buy the vehicle.

Hung: Status of a customer who's ready to sign the papers.

Hit a Home Run: Make a great deal of money on a particular sale.

Hosed 'em: Made some money on the deal.

Idiot light: A warning light on the instrument panel.

Juice: Money.

Junker: An old car ready for the scrap heap.

Key and a Heater: A basic car with no options.

Kickback: Money refunded to the car dealer after the sale is made. May come from the car maker, finance company or insurance companies from the sale of extended warranties.

Licking: When either the dealer or the customer loses money on a deal.

Loaded: A car with every option. A rich customer.

Long green: Money.

Lowball: An attempt to undercut another dealer's price.

Maypops: Bald tires.

Nickel: $500.

Numbers: The price of the vehicle.

Nut: The break-even point.

On the hood: Rebates, incentives, and special financing offered by a manufacturer or lender.

Pack: Money built into the price of the car to cover dealer's expenses (advertising & overhead in particular).

Pad: The amount of a sale meant for the salesman.

Player: A customer with a good credit history.

Pound: $1000.

Push: Cash, rebate, or special financing.

Qualify: Determine if the customer is ready to buy.

Rear-end money: Kickbacks and incentives given to a dealer by a lender for closing a financing deal.

Repo: A car that's repossessed for non-payment of a loan.

Ripley's Believe It Or Not: Obvious body damage poorly repaired.

Roach: A customer with a poor credit rating. A vehicle in need of a serious doll-up.

Roll 'em: Force exerted by a salesman to close a deal.

Rubberneck: A customer who has no intention of buying.

Shark: A ruthless, money-hungry salesman.

Short Arm: Very thrifty (cheap) customer.

Slam-dunk: Make a very profitable sale.

Sled: A slow and cumbersome vehicle. A worthless vehicle.

Snow job: An attempt to hide the truth from a customer with persuasive language.

Song and dance: An elaborate attempt to explain something to a customer.

Special financing: High-interest loans for customers with poor credit. Low-interest loans underwritten by the manufacturer.

Spiff: Bonus a salesperson receives if a sale is made.

Sticker shock: Customer's negative reaction to the price of the vehicle.

Stole It: Purchased a vehicle far below wholesale value.

Stroker: A customer who acts like they're ready to buy, and has no intention of doing so.

Sweep 'em: Don't waste any more time with a customer.

TD: Turned down. Usually refers to a customer's credit application.

Teaser: A basic car with few options (used to draw customers into the dealership).

Ticky Ticky: Vehicle with valve train noise.

Tin Lizzie: A very old vehicle.

Tire Kicker: Someone who doesn't have the money to buy, but looks just the same.

Took a Bath: Lost money on a deal.

Took a Pill: Lost a great deal of money on a deal.

Twist 'em: Force exerted by a salesman to close a deal.

Upside down: The car's true value is less than the amount owed on the vehicle. (Aka backwards)

www.ingramcontent.com/pod-product-compliance
Lightning Source LLC
Chambersburg PA
CBHW031648040426
42453CB00006B/243